PHalarope Books

PHalarope Books are designed specifically for the amateur naturalist. These volumes represent excellence in natural history publishing. Most books in the PHalarope series are based on a nature course or program at the college or adult education level or are sponsored by a museum or nature center. Each PHalarope Book reflects the author's teaching ability as well as writing ability. Among the books:

The Amateur Naturalist's Handbook
VINSON BROWN

Exploring Tropical Isles and Seas: An Introduction for the Traveler and Amateur Naturalist
FREDERIC MARTINI

A Field Guide to Personal Computers for Bird Watchers and Other Naturalists
EDWARD M. MAIR

A Field Guide to the Familiar: Learning to Observe the Natural World
GALE LAWRENCE

Insect Life: A Field Entomology Manual for the Amateur Naturalist
ROSS H. ARNETT, JR., and RICHARD L. JACQUES, JR.

A Natural History Notebook of North American Animals
NATIONAL MUSEUM OF NATURAL HISTORY, CANADA

Owls: An Introduction for the Amateur Naturalist
GORDON DEE ALCORN

Pond and Brook: A Guide to Nature Study in Freshwater Environments
MICHAEL CADUTO

Suburban Wildlife: An Introduction to the Common Animals of Your Back Yard and Local Park
RICHARD HEADSTROM

Thoreau's Method: A Handbook for Nature Study
DAVID PEPI

The Western Birdwatcher: An Introduction to Birding in the American West
KEVIN J. ZIMMER

The Wildlife Observer's Guidebook
CHARLES E. ROTH, Massachusetts Audubon Society

Wood Notes: A Companion and Guide for Birdwatchers
RICHARD H. WOOD/illustrations and commentary by Carol Decker

OWLS

An Introduction for the Amateur Naturalist

Gordon Dee Alcorn

PHalarope
Books

PRENTICE HALL PRESS
New York   London   Toronto   Sydney   Tokyo

The Robertson quote on page 116 is reprinted by permission of the editors of *The Condor* magazine and Mrs. Fletcher's letter is printed by permission of the Fletcher estate.

Published by Prentice Hall Press
A Division of Simon & Schuster, Inc.
Gulf + Western Building
One Gulf + Western Plaza
New York, New York 10023

PRENTICE HALL PRESS is a trademark of Simon & Schuster, Inc.

Originally published in different form as *Silent Wings* by Ye Galleon Press, Fairfield, Washington. Copyright © 1982 by Gordon Dee Alcorn.

Library of Congress Cataloging in Publication Data

Alcorn, Gordon Dee.
  Owls: an introduction for the amateur naturalist.

  (PHalarope books)
  Previously published as: Silent wings. © 1982.

  Bibliography: p. 163
  Includes index.
  1. Owls. 2. Title.
QL696.S8A43 1986   598'.97   85-16688
ISBN 0-13-647504-3

Manufactured in the United States of America

10 9 8 7 6 5 4 3

*To Rowena
for complete encouragement,
cooperation, and
dedication to my career*

CONTENTS

PREFACE

The American Ornithologists' Union recognizes eleven genera, twenty species, and fifty-seven races or sub-species of owls in North America. I make no attempt in this volume to compare or describe the characteristics of the races in any great detail. Sometimes differences are slight, and there may be occasions when ornithologists disagree on whether or not two populations are different or distinct enough to classify them separately. In the discussions of the birds that follow, some little attention is paid to the origins of the scientific names. A sentence or two about the person who first named the particular genus or species is also given. It is of interest to note how many of these names are originally given to certain owls many years ago and, also, how intimately many of the names are associated with the mythology of early Greece and Rome. For centuries owls have intrigued and ap-pealed to people. Their color, mien, behavior, and beauty ensure them an important, enduring, and unique place in natural history, and in the early days, some owls inspired thoughts of conservation.

Today we live in a vastly different world of nature from that of a century and more ago. That is why I make repeated reference to the writings of ornithologists who knew and studied owls before civilization modified the distribution and behavior of birds. In addition to emphasizing changes brought about in owl populations as a result of human encroachment into owl territory, I point out how the human's attitude toward raptors in general has changed. Modern evidence now shows that raptors are a valuable and necessary part of food chains. They should not be killed as "despised" birds merely because they eat other forms of life held valuable by humans. Typical of some early strong opinions regarding conservation are the words of Abbott [1888]:

> There can be no denial of the fact now established, that owls are eminently useful birds. That they occasionally destroy pigeons or poultry is of no significance considering the immense numbers of rats and mice that these birds devour. It will be years yet, probably, before the average farmer can be taught the truth about birds, and it would be of inestimable advantage to the country, and to all countries, if birds were protected in fact and not nominally. . . . The birds will have to take their chances until ignorance as to their value is finally overcome; and let us hope extinction will not overtake them before that happy time.

By making references to early times of ornithological literature, it is my thought that the interest and curiosity of readers might be stimulated to search out in various libraries, copies of old books hitherto unknown to many present-day readers. In addition, the quaint, florid writings of a century ago demonstrate a style seldom met with in this modern day.

It is both fascinating and revealing to study the pages of ornithological literature written by such men as Dawson, Bent, Coues, and others, revealing many quite obvious similarities in the behavior of birds today with those of many years ago. We can also learn of the harmful effects of human encroachment upon the habitats of owls. We can, for example, note that populations of owls today are smaller and are driven more and more into back country, away from civilization. In my boyhood, I could walk into the yard of my home in the countryside on almost any still, cool, quiet October evening and listen to the bell-like call of the Screech Owl within a few feet of the back fence. The Barn Owl, however, has accepted the structures of civilization for its nesting purposes to the point where only a minority of this species, in certain regions, can still be found in so-called natural sites such as cliffsides, holes in banks, and hollow trees. Also, this is one species of owl that has increased in population and has spread west and north in recent years.

I have attempted to standardize the format in the accounts of the various species. First comes the name of the bird, a few references to the origin of the name and to the designator, then a brief description of the plumages, distribution in North America, and the life cycle, including nestings and food habits.

Scattered throughout the treatment are some personal reminiscences. I have many of these because as a boy I lived in the country, and as a young man I became associated with several of America's fine ornithologists. We spent many years in the field looking at the birds. Also, as a young man I worked as a helper for a commercial taxidermist. In the five years of my employment with the taxidermist, we prepared many owls for the trophy rooms of sportsmen, although in those days the Barn Owl rarely appeared.

The following pages are not designed to function as a field guide; there are several good guides available today.

It is my hope that readers can learn about and learn to enjoy many characteristics of owls that are not described in a field guide.

My grateful thanks go to my wife, Rowena. Thanks, also, to Dr. Richard Fitzner, Ronald Karabaich, and Dale Thompson for their artwork, which reflects their skills in drawing, painting, and photography. And to Suzanne Barnett, Sandra Bauer, and Eileen McDowell, thanks for their continued interest in searching out references to enrich the manuscript, and for Eileen's willingness to spend many hours at the typewriter.

INTRODUCTION

Owls are unique among birds. All the species are distinctive in appearance and possess a singular beauty. They all have large heads, face masks, and forward-oriented eyes. The bill is large and hooked, and the feet are developed into long toes with sharp, curved nails (Figures 1 and 2). The character of the beak, the toes, and their diet of meat have led them to be classified as raptors. Sometimes they are called the "nocturnal birds of prey," but they are not like the other raptors, such as hawks, eagles, and falcons. Owls differ in anatomy, physiology, feather structure, and hunting techniques from other raptors. Most owls do not capture their prey in the air.

There has been an unusual surge of interest in the past couple of generations in observing birds, an interest popularly known as "bird watching." This interest largely centers around the identification of the species. But underlying this narrow interest is a realization that in addition to simply observing behavior, we are also

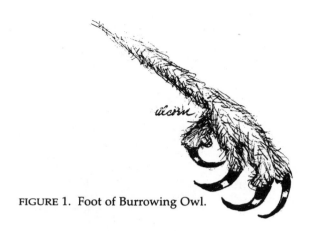

FIGURE 1. Foot of Burrowing Owl.

FIGURE 2. Foot of Snowy Owl.

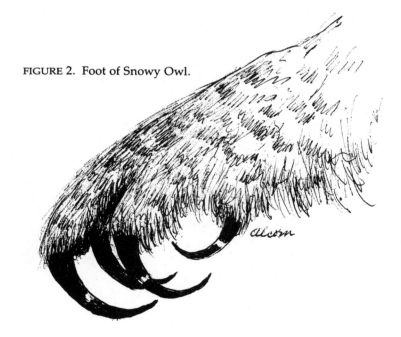

observing a most beautiful creature. There can be beauty of action, grace, and movement, but mostly we are observing the beauty of form, color, pattern, and feather design.

The feather is unique to birds. No other animal possesses a structure even remotely resembling the feather. Probably the most famous fossils ever discovered form a small series of fossil birds (*Archaeopteryx lithographica*) that were found in the Jurassic limestone of 140 million years ago in central Europe. Certainly no fossils have been studied more than these famous skeletons. There are five known examples of this bird, and each has feather imprints in the stone with the bony skeleton. Moreover, these fossil feathers show identical structures to those found in the feathers of modern birds. To date avian paleontologists have not been able to find any primitive precursor of the feather that could be labeled as an antecedent to the feather type found in *Archaeopteryx*. There has long been discussion among scientists in the world of paleontology about theories of the origin of feathers in birds, and the question has arisen many times: Have feathers, through processes of evolutionary selection, developed in the bird for purposes of flight or for purposes of heat retention? Feathers are light in weight, highly insulative, and strong, and through the eons of time a complex host of feather designs, patterns, and colors has developed in birds. Basically, when we observe birds, we are at least subconsciously admiring the feather complement of a species.

The feathers of owls are unusually soft, voluminous, flexible. The outer edges of the wing feathers, especially the primaries, are fimbriate. This tends to mute any sound that might be produced. The owls flight, as a result, is almost noiseless. This is necessary so that the bird may fly quietly toward its prey without

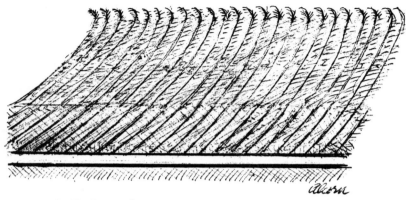

FIGURE 3. Fimbriae of owl feathers.

frightening it (Figure 3). All owls are completely clothed in feathers, except for the beak, eyes, ear openings, and in the Flammulated Screech Owl, the toes. Even the legs of most owls are covered with a thick blanket of feathers. Most species of owls have twelve tail feathers (a few have only ten). All species have eleven primaries.

One of the most outwardly distinguishing character-istics of all owls is the face mask, sometimes called the *disc*. The mask is formed by an arrangement of special feathers around the forward-looking eyes. In many owls this mask is round or oval in shape, with the feathers inside the periphery forming flat surfaces over which and on which sound waves from potential prey can be directed toward the ears. In the Barn Owl, the mask is heart-shaped (Figure 4). The periphery is formed by a ring of special, small, stiffened feathers. Inside the edges of the mask in all owls, many short, bristly feathers de-velop around the eye and over the base of the bill, point-ing forward so that the nostrils are covered, and leaving only the tip of the bill visible. The shape of the mask is

FIGURE 4. Face mask of Barn Owl.

simianlike in the Barn Owl, which gives this species the name of Monkey-faced Owl in some parts of the world. The feathers forming the outside of the disc of the Barn Owl are usually of a different color from all adjacent feathers, so that the face mask is always obvious and distinctive in this species. In the Snowy Owl, the face mask is marked by the bristly feathers rather than by dark, soft feathers.

Owls are built around their eyes, which are one of their most remarkable features (Figure 5). The eye is directed forward and is incapable of independent movement. Because it is fixed in the skull, owls must orient themselves by rotating the head. Some species can turn their heads up to 270 degrees. Most owls are nocturnal

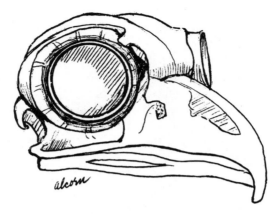

FIGURE 5. Skull of Great Horned Owl showing fixity of eye sockets. Life size.

or crepuscular, yet they have excellent vision in daylight. Big species of owls possess an eye larger than the human eye. With this enormous structure and a correspondingly large pupil, owls hunt successfully even in dim light. In the eyes of most birds there is a bony ring surrounding the pupil and the anterior portion of the eye called the *sclera*. In the owl the sclera develops into a tube and thereby unites the lens, the iris, and the cornea with the retina, which is located in the posterior part of the eye. With the visual structures of the owl eye held captive in a bony tube, efficiency of focus declines. Partly to compensate for this handicap, the lens in the owl eye is soft and easily modified in thickness, giving the eye a more flexible power of accommodation. Even so, owls cannot focus their eyes on objects that are too close, so that in order to pounce upon their prey they must be at enough distance away from it to develop a sharp focus in their eyes. There may be a slight forward and backward movement of the retina to aid in this acuity of focus. Smooth muscles change the curvature of the cornea, the outermost membrane in the owl eye, to aid in accommodating the eye to proper focus. In addition, other smooth muscles are used to exert pressure on the lens to alter its shape to aid in establishing sharp focus. In most owls the iris is bright yellow, but in a few it is brown.

There is a third "eyelid," or nictitating membrane, called the *nictitans,* over the eyes of owls. The nictitans is opaque in owls but is transparent in other birds. The function of the nictitans in owls is not thoroughly understood. At one time it was thought to be a structure that would cleanse the eyeball, but no proof of this has ever been shown. Also, it was once thought to close over the eye to restrict the entrance of strong light. This theory, too, has fallen out of favor, since artificial light applied to the front of the owl eye does not always cause the nictitans to cover the eyeball. As do humans, owls lower the upper lid in the blinking reflex, but unlike humans they raise the lower lid when sleeping.

No bird has an external appendage relating to the sense of hearing. Many owls have tufts of feathers that resemble ears growing from the top of the skull directly above the eyes. The vernacular names of several owls refer to these feather arrangements by including the word "eared"—for example, Long-eared Owl and Short-eared Owl. These tufts, called *plumicorns,* have nothing to do with ears or the auditory sense in owls. The owls that possess plumicorns can move these structures at will and do so in varying circumstances. The Long-eared Owl, for example, completely depresses the ear tufts during anxiety.

The auditory sense in all owls is well developed. There is an ear opening on each side of the skull covered with small feathered flaps that can close over the ear channel completely (Figures 6a and 6b). It is a strik-

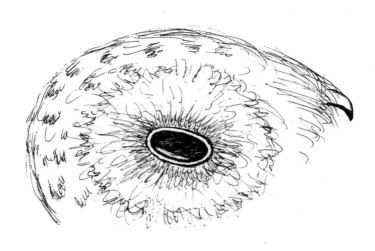

FIGURE 6a. Right ear openings of Snowy Owl, above, and Short-eared Owl, below. Life size. Note how the right ear opening is lower in the skull than the left. Compare with Figure 6b.

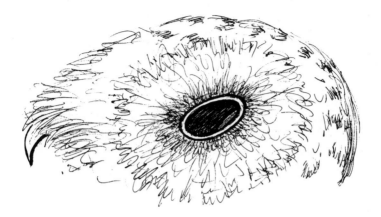

FIGURE 6b. Left ear openings of Snowy Owl, above, and Short-eared Owl, below. Life size. Note the large ear flap in the Short-eared Owl. Compare with Figure 6a.

ing fact that in many species the two ear openings of an individual owl differ markedly from one another in both size and shape. In several owl species one ear opening is also higher on the skull than the other (Figure 7). The left ear opening tends to be oval or round and larger than the right. The right ear opening may be slitlike and somewhat angular. Sound waves coming from the left, therefore, tend to create a louder response in the auditory part of the brain than those coming from the right. When the flaps are lifted and the auditory canal is open, the bird can pick up the faintest sounds by turning its head in the direction of the sound. It is noticeable that owls ranging over a field searching for food use a more or less constant back-and-forth movement of the head. Great Gray Owls, with their acute sense of hearing, are thus able to locate a gopher in a shallow burrow and can retrieve it by thrusting a foot into the burrow.

The face mask in owls, which serves to create a comparatively wide distance between the two ear openings, also aids in development of acuity. If the head is oriented toward the source of the sound, one ear may receive the stimulus a fraction of a second sooner than the other ear. This helps the bird to determine the direction of the sound and adds to its efficiency in capturing

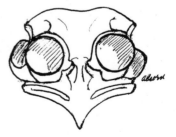

FIGURE 7. Skull of Pygmy Owl showing asymmetrical ear openings and placement on the skull.

prey by locating delicate sound in twilight or darkness when prey is scarcely visible. Repeated hearing experiments with Barn Owls show that this species can home in on and capture moving prey in total darkness. The slight sounds made by the moving prey are sufficient to lead the owl directly to it.

The size of the ear opening in various species of owls reflects the habitat and the terrain to which these several species have become highly adapted. The Snowy Owl, native to the tundra of the northland, has a comparatively small auditory canal, whereas the Short-eared Owl, one quarter the size and weight, has a much larger auditory apparatus. The tundra is soft and quiet, and it would be quite difficult for even a sharp-eared owl to hear a tundra rodent chewing on grass stems. Therefore, the Snowy Owl sits motionless for long hours on the summit of a hummock in the rolling terrain. Its keen eyes can detect the slightest movement of the prey animal. The Short-eared Owl commonly inhabits the grassland and the dune areas, in which its prey are more or less hidden. The owls can actually hear the voles and field mice gnawing on the dry grass stems. Some owls have indeed become adapted to hunt with their ears or with their eyes.

The bone arrangement in owls shows the usual structural adaptations of the skeleton that are observed in most other birds. In size, owls are deceptive. They look larger than they are because of a thick covering of soft feathers. When one views the skeleton, the legs and wings appear to be out of proportion with the size of the body. This is especially true of the rib cage that surrounds the thoracic and visceral organs, which appears to be too small when compared with the large legs and wings (Figures 8 and 9). The humerus (upper arm) is almost as long as the lower arm, which is composed of the radius-ulna. The lower leg (drumstick) is formed by

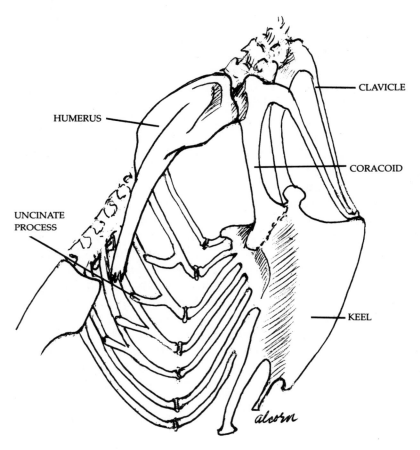

FIGURE 8. Rib cage of Great Horned Owl. Note narrow clavicles.

the fusion of the tibia and fibula into one strong bone; the fibula is fused almost its entire length. These bones need to be long and strong, as they support large muscles and tendons which facilitate owls' movement and flexibility for grasping prey with their powerful talons.

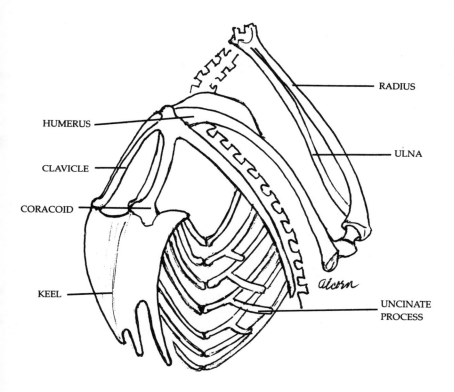

FIGURE 9. Rib cage of Pygmy Owl. Note long uncinate processes.

But in most owls these appendages do not appear to be outsize, since the numerous feathers, as many as 10,000 in some species, typically fluff out around the body, giving the living bird a more normal appearance.

Because the wings are large, bones in the pectoral area around the rib cage must be sturdy and rigid (see Figure 8). The coracoid process (bone) that connects sternum to shoulder in owls is unusually well developed

and is anchored solidly to the sternum, with little flexibility with the sternum. The clavicles (furculum) make a
second connection of shoulder to sternum (in upper arm
area), loosely attached in most owls but tightly fused in
the Barn Owl. In effect, the shoulder area in birds (well
developed in owls) consists of a double pectoral girdle.
During flight, the resulting rigidity and strength (without loss of flexibility) prevent loss of energy developed
by the wings to be transferred to the body. The sternum
and keel are comparatively small, being only about two
thirds the length of the humerus. The rib cage tends to
be small but very flexible. The uncinate processes of the
ribs are well developed, especially in the smaller species
of owls (Figure 9). To provide more strength, the clavicle
is widened into a keel-like process on the upper end,
which gives much more surface for wing-muscle attachment. Most owls are strong flyers.

Since owls must seek their prey on the ground,
many species fly to and fro over an open area. The wing
beat may be regularly interrupted by short periods of
sailing. A few species are capable of hovering; in the case
of the Barn Owl this hovering period may last as long as
one minute. Because of the relatively small body and
disproportionately large wings, owls appear to be unusually buoyant. Some owls, such as the Short-eared and
Burrowing, range over an open field or dune area giving
the appearance of erratic flight punctuated by momen-
tary disappearances on the ground, only to reappear
with prey in their talons. Since many owls capture prey
of considerable size and weight compared to their own
weight, there must be a reserve of strength in the hunting bird to accommodate wing load. The small body and
large wingspread make possible relatively slow flight
without danger of stalling when the bird is hunting.
When the hunting owl captures its prey, the weight of

the animal taken must not exceed the reserve of wing-load capacity of the hunter. Wing loading is the ratio of surface area of wings (not tail) to weight of bird. A small Barn Owl may use all of its reserve of strength in wing displacement to capture and return to the nest with a large rat clutched in its talons. A Screech Owl may successfully bring home a small rabbit. I have never seen a Great Horned Owl actually carrying a skunk in its talons, but, as will be mentioned later, skunks obviously are a favorite article of diet of this species. On the ground, a Barn Owl can run and jump and will do so like a cat if the first strike with its talons misses the target. This species has no trouble becoming airborne from the ground with prey firmly clutched by one or both feet. Since owls feed on other animals that they must catch, all of their physical structures must be adapted to discovering and capturing their living prey.

Owls are completely carnivorous. They feed upon such varieties of foods as insects, frogs, salamanders, fish, snakes, mammals, and other birds. A few owls, such as the Snowy Owl, will feed on carrion. Since the owl has no crop, food must begin to be digested in the gizzard. The flesh and the soft parts of the food eaten are partially digested and passed into the intestine for absorption. Owls have a low acid level in the gizzard. Therefore, the hair, feathers, and bones of the food cannot be digested or even softened so that digestion of these hard parts could be carried on when they are passed into the intestine. These indigestible parts of the food are passed forward from the gizzard into the *proventriculus*, which is the true stomach of the bird. They remain in the proventriculus until they are rolled into a small, ball-like bolus and regurgitated as pellets (Figure 10). Pellet regurgitation in owls appears to be voluntary rather than a simple reflex function. There are several

FIGURE 10. Owl pellets. Note fur and bones of small mammal prey.

hundred species of birds known to be pellet ejectors, but the efficiency of the process is probably as high in owls as it is in any other bird.

An examination of an owl's pellets is always fruitful in determining the diet of the bird. The skulls, bones, and feathers of small mammals and birds that might be the size of a mouse or a sparrow are often regurgitated whole and unbroken (Figure 11).

The amount of food that an owl can consume during its feeding period is remarkable. A single Barn Owl will eat one and a half times its own weight in mice or rats in one evening. Obviously, this is less nutritive than might appear at first glance, since all hair, bones, and feathers do not contribute to the caloric needs of the owl. But it is still a comparatively enormous amount of food.

In general, a laboratory examination of owl pellets can yield important information about prey populations. In addition to learning what species of prey are in the pellets, researchers can fairly accurately determine dates concerning the number of litters born to prey in a season and when these litters are born. Regular collections will also show the approximate age of maturity of the prey. Interpretation of the statistics derived from pellet analysis, however, can be misleading. For example, the dominant mouse species in pellets may not necessarily be the dominant prey population within the owl's feeding territory. First, the relative sizes of the individuals within the prey species may account for their relative abundance in the diet. Obviously, more mammals of lesser weight must be eaten to fulfill the needs of the diet. Thus, one might be led to a false conclusion. If a pellet analysis showed two shrews for every mouse, the owl may derive the same amount of energy from the two shrews as it could secure from only one mouse. It may also be the case that the owl is more adept at securing one species than it is another species.

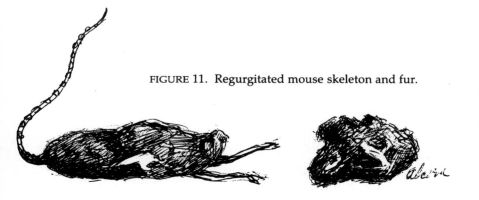

FIGURE 11. Regurgitated mouse skeleton and fur.

Second, the ability of the hunting owl to secure its items of food may be highly influenced by terrain or habitat. Voles, for instance, may conceal themselves better in grass than do mice. In this case, the owl may have no particular choice and is merely selecting that item that is most easily secured. Owls may also arbitrarily choose one prey item over another. There is some evidence, secured by observation and research, that owls may be somewhat selective based on the taste of the prey. Bunn and others (1982) point out that while the subterranean mole is not an abundant item in the diet of the Barn Owl, moles—when selected—are usually left untouched after a bite or two.

Third, attempts to compare prey population numbers caught in traps with numbers indicated by pellet analyses may not reveal true population numbers or the favorite dietary items of the owl. It has been shown repeatedly that some species of small mammals are easier to lure into a trap than others. Consequently, if one species was trapped in a two-to-one ratio over another species over a large enough number of trap nights, it may simply show that the one easier to trap has not learned to avoid traps!

Fourth, some research seems to point out that some owls can select prey on the basis of sound rather than sight. It may be possible for certain owls to identify the squeaks—maybe ultrasounds—given off by particular prey items. Furthermore, some little research has led to the possibility that owls, using the auditory sense, can home in on the sounds made by a small rodent sitting in the grass, chewing on the stems.

Pellet analysis is often valuable, however, in qualitatively identifying a prey population. On a number of occasions, skulls and other bones picked up by an owl in its territory have proven to be a valid addition to the prey checklists of the region. Owls are efficient at finding the prey items in their territories. A number of years ago, a road-kill Horned Owl was brought to our museum as a specimen to be added to our collection. While strictly speaking not a pellet item, nonetheless the two coiled garter snakes in the owl's gizzard were determined to be of a sub-species unknown on the isolated island where the owl was secured. Bunn and others (1982), quoting Glue and Morgan (1977), further state that, while not a major source of information, the pellets of some owls have been found to contain aluminum bands placed on the legs of birds of species undergoing migration research.

Pellet analysis may also indicate at what time of day certain prey species are consumed. For example, a Barn Owl may hunt early in the evening, rest in the dead of night, and after a few hours expel a pellet. Then this same individual might hunt again in the early dawn, digest this second meal of the day, and perhaps expel a second pellet by midday or afternoon. A species analysis of the pellets might show different populations of prey animals abroad at different times of the day. (French ornithologists, who have done much research on the Barn Owl, with the exactness of their language designate the first expelled pellet *pellote nocturne* and the second one *pellote diurne*.)

Owls exhibit a great range in size. The tiny Elf Owl of the southwest desert of America is the smallest in North America, and the Great Horned is the largest. Head-to-tail measurements and weights of some common owls—small, medium, large—are shown in Table 1.

The Eagle Owl of northern Africa, Europe, and Asia will reach a length of about 75 centimeters and weigh up to 3584 grams.

Owls are distributed all over the world and are found on most continents except Antarctica and on some of the oceanic islands in the Pacific. Falla and others

Table 1

Owl	A.O.U.#	Measurement from Head to Tail (in cm.)	Weigh (in g.)
Elf	381	11-13	40
Screech	373	20-22	Variable up to 200
Great Horned	375	52-58	Variable up to 2000

(1966) state that the Barn Owl is the most widely distributed land bird in the world.

There is little paleontological data on modern owls. There are North American early fossils that are at least sixty million years old, attesting to the antiquity of owls. Rich and Bohaska (1976) state that a Paleocene tarsometatarsus from southwestern Colorado is from the oldest known owl, which probably provides a link between barn owls and typical owls. Feduccia (1980) refers to a Pleistocene flightless Barn Owl from Cuba. The tarsometatarsus of this fossil measures over twice the length of the same bone in the modern Horned Owl. This measurement would make the fossil bird over three feet tall. Arrendondo (1976) suggests that the Owlet-frogmouth of Australia, New Guinea, and New Caledonia might show a link between modern owls and fossil *Caprimulgiformes*. These Owlet-frogmouths, sometimes called Moth Owls, resemble owls in their hooked bills, feet, diet, and feeding techniques. While the Owlet-frogmouth feeds on insects on the wing, it also picks its food from the ground, as do true owls. The committee on Classification and Nomenclature of the American Ornithologists' Union, which prepares the various editions of the *Check-List of North American Birds,* has recognized for many years the possible phylogenetic relationships between owls and goatsuckers by placing these two orders back to back in the published check-lists. Suggestions have also been made that a paleontological link may exist between modern owls and a primitive ancestral form in the Ardeidae (herons) in the Ciconiformes since modern herons and Barn Owls both possess a pectinate middle claw (Figure 12). This last "evidence" is certainly nebulous, as most ornithologists ascribe no particular meaning to the rare appearance of a pectinate claw in birds. A few students of birds, however, state that the claw is probably used to groom the face mask.

The fossil evidence relating modern birds to primitive ancestors in many orders of birds is too scanty to be conclusive. The fact that modern owls *(Strigiformes)* have talons and a hooked beak for tearing flesh, as do hawks, eagles, and falcons *(Falconiformes)* does not necessarily point to a common paleontological ancestry between these two groups. (They were placed in the 1910 *Checklist* in one order, Raptores.) The anatomical features of feet, bill, and diet in owls and hawks show convergent evolution rather than a commonality of ancestry. To be sure, owls as a group do not feed on the wing as do most members of the *Falconiformes,* but the carnivorous features are present in both. Because of the many extreme adaptations that have been brought about in owls through evolution over a long period of time and in a

FIGURE 12.
Pectinate middle claw of Barn Owl.

great variety of habitats, there are today twenty-eight recognized genera and approximately 150 species in the world.

Perhaps no other bird group can be found in so many diverse habitats. Owls live from the frozen northern tundra to the hot deserts. There are populations in the deep boreal forests, in the thick, temperate rain forests, and in the tropical forests. Some owls prefer to be active in and around human civilization. Most owls, worldwide, are not highly migratory. However, the northern populations of some species of owls are somewhat migratory. Those that breed in the northland may winter in the southern United States and Mexico. Specific habitats within latitudinal boundaries influence the lightness or darkness of the plumages, so that because of the more or less limited migratory behavior, light northern races frequently mingle with darker coastal forms during winter months.

The nesting season depends somewhat on the latitude occupied by the bird. The Horned Owls and the Snowy Owls in northern latitudes begin their nesting activities in March or perhaps April, when the country is still under the spell of the cold. It is an inspiring experience to walk through the northland on a crisp, clear, still, cold night and to listen to the hooting calls of the owls as they commune with each other. There may be snow on the ground and little owls in the nest.

Owls do not build their own nests but will try to find an abandoned nest of another species, such as a hawk, or crow, or magpie. The Barn Owl uses the rafters of a barn, attic, or belfry of a church or other large building. Snowy Owls and Short-eared Owls nest on the ground. Many owl species prefer a hollow area in a dark place. The Burrowing Owl nests underground in the tunnel or hole of a ground squirrel, prairie dog, or other prairie animal.

All owl eggs, like those of many birds nesting in cavities, are white and tend to be roundish. The eggs of a few species, however, such as the Boreal, Short-eared, Long-eared, Great Gray, and Snowy Owls, tend to be oval. Clutch sizes will vary from two to six in the larger species of owls and from three to seven in the smaller species. Species that live and breed in the cold, northern climates have time to raise only one brood per season. In temperate and warmer climates some species may raise a second brood, provided prey species are sufficient over the period of time that the young are hatched and fledged. In tropical climates, owls are not dependent upon seasons to complete their annual life cycle. Incubation takes several weeks, and owls, like many birds, begin to incubate as soon as the first egg is laid. Since eggs are laid at intervals, the young hatch at intervals.

In most species of owls, both male and female share the tasks of incubating and feeding. Incubation requires little active behavior by the parents. This situation changes dramatically when there are one or more owls in the nest demanding to be fed. The clutch of three or more young owls in the nest requires an almost feverish gathering of food to supply their needs. In good seasons, when lower temperatures are not a factor and there has been a high build-up of prey items, two hunting parents can keep up with the demands of hungry owlets. On cold nights, voles, mice, and other prey tend to be less active and therefore more difficult to search out and carry home. Prolonged periods of rain also create great difficulty for marauding parents. Many owls require considerable hunting territory, perhaps covering as much as one square mile. If prey populations are at their nadir or even less abundant than normal, parents expend considerable energy ranging over their territory. Clutch size itself may be partially governed by the quantity of food items available. In years when the vole population is larger than normal, owl clutch size also tends to be higher. Better and more food available to the adult female tends to dictate a larger clutch. With five young in a nest and plenty of food items in the field, the feeding adults will obviously be less pushed to return prey to five hungry owlets than to feed three where prey species are widely scattered. This is nature at her cybernetic best: when prey items are found in abundance, increased enrichment of owl diet results in larger egg sets. This means more hunting with resultant decreases in the prey populations.

Small prey items are fed whole to young owls in the nest soon after hatching, perhaps even before the young owls' eyes are open. In quite a number of species of owls, the hen will straddle the chick from the rear and dangle the food in front of the chick's beak so the food touches the bristles of the chick. In the early days of feeding (the white-down stage), the adult usually pulls pieces of meat from the prey and offers it to the owlet. This consists usually of pure meat without feathers, bones, or hair so that there is no pellet formation in the early stages of growth of young owls. Later on, large items of prey are fought over and dismembered by the young. This means that in years when food is scarce, those young birds that hatch from the eggs at the end of the incubation period are often too weak to survive in the nest because they are not able to compete with their older nestlings for food. Ornithologists do not agree that this is a normal way for nature to "weed out" the weakest. Observations made on nestling owls (especially the Barn Owl) have led some ornithologists to believe that some cannibalism might exist. Research has shown that in times of hunger young owls in the nest will eat a dead one of the clutch. It is not agreed that the victim will be deliberately killed to be eaten. It is eaten only after death due to starvation. Some adults eat the shells of hatchlings.

Unlike most birds in higher orders, owls do not excrete feces in mucoid bags. In orders of birds where this physiological process is common, the adult may eat the sac or carry it away to be dropped some distance from the nest. Young owls, sitting on a ledge of a barn rafter, tree nest, or cliffside, tend to defecate over the edge of the nest. Where this is not possible, nest sanitation becomes a problem. Barn Owls in Europe have been enticed into an artificial nest box for nesting and rearing young with some success. In this situation, nest hygiene has been downgraded. In most nesting situations, however, nest sanitation is not a serious problem.

Young owls newly hatched from the egg are covered with white down and are blind. After about a week, the white down is usually replaced with a darker coat, and eyes and ears begin to open. Fledging may take up to several months, but by the autumn of the year the young bird has grown all of its adult feathers and has reached its full size. A partial molt may occur in the early spring following hatching, and during the first summer a complete molt will bring the bird to adulthood. Most owls are able to breed at the age of one year, but life expectancy is comparatively short. There are records of a few reaching the age of twenty years, but only in captivity. An old owl in the wild may reach nine or ten years of age.

Through the centuries, owls have intrigued the imaginations of humans, being associated with wisdom, victory, good luck, bad luck, confusion, abomination, fear, ill omen, disaster, doom, and with other animals such as the dragon. For many centuries they have been regarded as creatures of the night. Because of these associations and because of their mysterious voices, legends, stories, and beliefs have built up relating owls to mystery, certain events, and myths. Some owls influenced the cultural and social practices of early civilizations. In Asia, reverence for the Barn Owl historically dates from the time of Genghis Khan, the founder of the Empire of Tartary. A legend holds that Genghis, fleeing from his enemies, took refuge in a small grove of trees. A Barn Owl settled on a bush nearby, persuading the pursuers that no man could conceal himself so near to a perching owl. To the present day certain tribes of the region, on holidays and festivals, are said to wear a plume of Barn Owl feathers on their heads as tribute to the bird that saved Genghis. The owl has been used as a symbol for many groups, such as sororities and fraternities. It is even used as a trademark for certain products for sale in the marketplace.

The various songs of owls, coming perhaps in the dead of night, make profound impressions upon the listener. Owls are capable of giving voice to a variety of sounds, variously described as hooting, screaming, chittering, wailing, and squeaking. A few owls have onomatopoeic names such as Screech Owl, Laughing Owl (of Australia), Barking Owl (of Australia and southeast Asia), and Saw-whet Owl. In the first three of these, "songs" are self-evident. The "song" of the Saw-whet supposedly mimics the sound of a file sharpening the teeth of a saw. All owl species exhibit a variety of songs. During the breeding season, for example, the Saw-whet Owl may hold forth for hours—even in the nighttime— with a continuous, lilting crescendo of a musical note, somewhere between what could be called a chirp or short whistle and a bell-like sound. The most common song of the Screech Owl is not a screech at all but a very musical note rising in the scale with increasing tempo. The songs of owls vary in frequency and intensity within the yearly cycle. There may be a variety of sounds demonstrating alarm, warning, fear, and courtship. Samuels (1872) describes several owls

making "night hideous with their discordant, mournful cries." Never shall I forget a serenade I once had the pleasure of hearing in the State of Maine, in which this bird (the Great Horned Owl) maintained the basso. We were encamped on the shores of Lake Umbagog: our tent was pitched on a bluff overlooking the lake, and behind us was the deep, dark forest of pines and hemlocks. We had just got fairly in to our first nap, the sweet follower of our day's toils, when we were awakened by the hootings of one of these owls, "Waugh, hoo, hoo, hoo!" or "Who cooks for you?" as the Western traveller understood it, which seemed to be addressed to us from a tree almost over our tent. We listened: presently another took up the theme, and then both together. They had scarcely finished their duet, when, from away up the lake, came the shrill, mournful cry or scream of the Loon: this was continued and answered by others, until, with owls and loons, the night was vocal with melodious sounds. After this had died away, and all was still, there came from a bush near our tent the almost heavenly song of the White-throated Sparrow, the "Nightingale of the North." One cannot imagine the effect produced by the contrast: he must be on the spot in the dark night, and, through the sighing of the winds amid the grand old trees, hear the owls and loons; then, silence, broken by the beautiful song of the Nightingale.

Abbott (1888), quite a figure in his day, with characteristic vigor says of the Barred Owl and its voice,

its terrible voice, that has been well described as like the forced laugh of a maniac. Dr. Brewer says that it is the female only that gives utterance to the horricapillatory screams mentioned, and the male is subdued in all that he says. Good! and such things are not unknown beyond the pale of owldom.

Vocalizations emanate in birds from the syrinx, which is developed at the junction of the two bronchial tubes and the trachea. In most birds the syrinx is an elaborate structure formed of thin bone with membranes stretched across windows, forming an irregular, drumlike organ. Air emitted from the lungs and swirling about in the syrinx sets up vibrations resulting in sound. In owls the syrinx is much less complex and is formed of incomplete cartilaginous rings in the bronchi (Figure 13). Air passing rapidly through the bronchi develops vibrations in the membranes between the bronchial rings. Varieties of sounds and modulations of sound are brought about by the speed at which air is expelled from the lungs and by changes in the mouth and throat, resulting in changes in pitch and timbre. This type of sound-producing mechanism is found in a few other orders of birds, including the *Caprimulgiformes.* This might point to another small item of evidence of a relationship between owls and frogmouths.

Many birds produce sounds that do not come from the voice box or syrinx. In some species of owls, surprisingly, there is a wing clapping. This results when the bird takes off rapidly from a perch or from the ground. It appears during the downbeat or at the apex of the downbeat. The tips of the primaries actually touch, producing the typical clapping sound. It is commonly heard in pigeons and some other birds that need speed at the takeoff. Owls also, during occasions of ·anxiety or fear, practice a bill clapping that denotes aggression. The two bills coming smartly together produce such a sound,

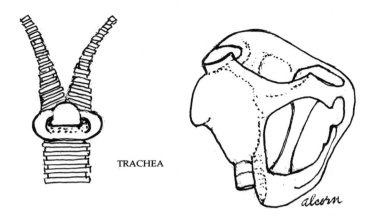

TRACHEA

FIGURE 13. Voice boxes of Barn Owl, left, and American Merganser, right. Note small size of the voice structure in the owl.

which might intimidate an animal that threatens the owl. Bill clapping is very commonly heard in immature owls as they fight over food in the nest. Very often in owls there is a hissing sound formed by air passing over the beak rapidly at the same time that the clapping of the beak is heard. The hissing apparently adds to the threat in times of confrontation with an opponent that has inspired fear in the owl.

In Greek and Roman mythology the owl is dedicated to Minerva, who was recognized as the patroness of intellect. On ancient Athenian coins dating back 2500 years B.C., the owl is used to signify victory, luck, and wisdom. Here—as has happened before—the owl is depicted on a coin and alongside a spray from an olive tree. Together these signify peace and prosperity, the aspira tions and the interests of the Athenian state. On the reverse side of these coins is the head of Athena, the goddess of wisdom. In the fifth century, the owl appeared on the Greek tetradrachum coin. Today, birds appearing on modern coins are used to typify the owl fauna of a particular country. The Micmac Indian tribe of New Brunswick told how the Snowy Owl lamented the end of the golden age of the amity of humans and animals.

References to the owl are legion throughout literature. In Shakespeare's *Macbeth*, preceding the murder of Duncan, it is reported that "On Tuesday last, a falcon towering in her pride of place, was a mousing owl hawked at and killed," and when Macbeth exclaims to Lady Macbeth, "I have done the deed. Dids't thou not hear a noise?" she answers, "I heard the owl scream." Gray, in his "Elegy Written in a Country Church Yard," writes that:

> *Save that from yonder ivy'mantled tow'r*
> *The mopeing owl does to the moon complain*
> *Of such, as wand'ring near her secret bow'r,*
> *Molest her ancient solitary reign.*

In The *Aeneid*, sometime between 29 B.C. and 19 B.C., Virgil wrote, "...the voice of that husband calling upon her. There was something dirge-like, too, in the tones of the owl on the roof-top." Alfred Tennyson sang of the owl. Dossi depicts animals that were once the lovers of the island enchantress Circe. One of them was an owl.

Superstitions have arisen about owls throughout the centuries. The poultryman believed that owls were responsible for adversely affecting production of poultry, thus causing loss and damage. On the other hand, most farmers regard owls as assets in controlling destructive rodents about the farmlands. Many states now protect most owls by law; the exception is usually the Great Horned Owl, which is still regarded as troublesome in taking poultry and even the farmer's cat. The priests in the early mission days in California had a special interest in the Barn Owl. In Minot (1877), Dr. Brewer says:

> The propensity of the California bird to drink the sacred oil of the consecrated lamps about the altars of the Missions was frequently referred to by the priests, whenever any allusion was made to this Owl.

There are numerous Biblical references to the owl. Isaiah especially used the owl to point up the dangers to man and his association with this bird. In Isaiah 34:11, there are two references. One says:

> The owl also and the raven shall dwell in it, and he shall stretch out upon it the line of confusion and the stones of emptiness.

And again:

> There shall the great owl make her nest and lay and hatch and gather under her shadow. There shall vultures also be gathered everyone with her mate.

In Isaiah 13:21:

> But wild beasts of the desert shall lie there and their houses shall be full of dole creatures. Owls shall dwell there and satyrs shall dance there.

In Isaiah 43:20:

> The beasts of the field shall honor me, the dragons and the owls.

In Deuteronomy 14:16, which outlines the laws of behavior, we read:

> Of all clean birds shall ye eat. But these are they of which ye shall not eat; and the owl and the night hawk and the cuckoo and the hawk after his kind. And the little owl and the great owl.

Job 30:29 says:

> I am brother to dragons and a companion to owls.

In Leviticus 11:7, 18, the people are again warned:

> These are they which ye shall not eat and the owl and the little owl and the cormorant and the great owl.

Psalm 102:6 sings of the birds:

> I am like a pelican in the wilderness. I am like an owl of the desert.

There are more appearances of owls in fairly modern literature. The most lighthearted reference to the owl in modern literature occurs in Edward Lear's "The Owl and the Pussycat." This probably is the most unlikely combination ever to set sail in a "beautiful pea-green boat."

OWL FAMILIES

There are two owl families in the world. These consist of the Barn Owls and a group commonly called Typical Owls (*Strigidae*).

Barn Owls belong to the family *Tytonidae* and are divided into two genera totaling eleven species worldwide. Outside of North America, true Barn Owls are found in Africa, southern China, Australia, the Celebes Islands, Madagascar, New Britain, and New Guinea. Recently, a few specimens have also been discovered in New Zealand. The Barn Owl was introduced to the main islands of Hawaii in recent years, and it is now well established there. Falla (1966) states that the Barn Owl is probably the most widely distributed land bird in the world. In addition, the Barn Owl might be the most beneficial of all the world's birds.

Barn Owls appear knock-kneed when they stand due to the fact that the intertarsel joints in the lower leg bend toward each other. The heart-shaped facial mask in

Barn Owls is well developed (see Figure 4). The iris of the eye is brown. In the true owls, or Typical Owls (Strigidae), the inner toe is much shorter than the middle, but in the Barn Owls the inner toe and the middle toe are approximately the same length. The fourth toe in Barn Owls has an unusual feature; it is so flexible that it can be directed forward or backward. The serration that develops as a tiny comb along one edge of the middle toe of the Barn Owl does not appear in Typical Owls. This comb may serve to groom the disc feathers or the bristles around the bill. Its use, however, has not been authenticated.

The internal skeletal parts of the Barn Owl show some differences from those of the true or Typical Owls. One obvious difference is shown in the furculum, or wishbone. This structure, in Barn Owls, is firmly attached at its base to the upper point of the sternum. In the Strigidae, the furculum is not fused with the sternum. The outer pair of tail feathers is longest in Barn Owls, which is the reverse of that condition in Typical Owls.

There are twenty-four genera and more than 130 species in the Strigidae. Typical Owls, unlike Barn Owls, have no "comb" on the middle claw and usually have a yellow iris and a rounded facial disk. While perching, Typical Owls do not present the appearance of being long-legged and awkwardly knock-kneed.

In North America there is one species of Barn Owl, but there are ten genera and perhaps as many as eighteen species of Typical Owls.

COMMON BARN OWL
Tyto alba (Scopoli)

Tyto is a Greek word for a species of owl. *Alba*—
"white"—is Latin and is given to this species because of
the large number of white feathers on the body of the
bird. The Barn Owl is medium-sized, measuring approximately 38 to 40 cm (15 to 16 in.), and weighs approximately 330 g (12 ounces), with the females about 50 g
heavier. Barn Owls have twelve tail feathers and eleven
primaries, but the eleventh primary is vestigal; it is hidden in the coverts and is difficult to see. The plumage is

35

soft and gold in color. The back is spotted or streaked with white or gray. Ornithologists have wondered why a bird as white as the Barn Owl has not, through many generations of natural selection, become dark. Bunn and others (1982) speculate that the white plumage of the Barn Owl is a result of selective factors for better conceal-ment in the white chalk country of prehistoric Great Brit-ain. With the coming of civilization and increased human population, many of the open fields in England have given way to man-made structures such as barns, which the owl has found readily adaptable for nesting. Accept-ance of civilization—now widespread in the world—has not, through natural selection, changed to any extent the whitish plumage of the Barn Owl to a darker dress. The undersurface is buff or white, and it is also spotted or barred with white or gray. The wings and tail are barred, and the facial mask is long and heart-shaped. The Barn Owl is sometimes called the Golden Owl or the Monkey-faced Owl because of the color and shape of the face mask. The bill is long and concealed by stiff feathers around the nostrils. Compared to other species, the eyes in the Barn Owl are relatively small and brown. It has long legs, completely but sparsely covered with feathers as are the toes, and it has long claws that are hooked and sharp.

Giovanni Antonio Scopoli, who first named this bird, was an Italian physician and natural scientist born in Cavalese in June 1723. Educated in Austria, he went on to become, at various times in his life, a professor of minerology and natural history, the first physician to the Austrian miners in Tyrol, and the author of many natural history publications. He died in Pavia in 1788.

The Barn Owl is a resident of North America from approximately south of the United States border with Canada. A few stragglers are found as far north as southeast Alaska. To the south, the Barn Owl is found all over America, and into Mexico and the islands of the West Indies. It also inhabits the islands in the Gulf of California. It is largely nocturnal, solitary in habit, and non-migratory. Migration is seen, however, in a few of the northern populations. Some of these populations along the northern border of the United States and the southern border of Canada move southward in the wintertime, apparently to seek a warmer climate.

The wings of many birds have their primaries tapered toward their ends. Such primaries are said to be *emarginate*. Emarginate primaries are commonly found in soaring birds and birds that fly long distances (Figure 14). When a bird such as a hawk or an eagle is soaring, emargination allows the tips of the primaries to separate so that the air can spill through them and thus reduce friction and turbulence. In most owls, the primaries are not narrowed and therefore not emarginate but constantly overlap so that the tips of the primaries are truncate. This arrangement is highly developed in Barn Owls (Figure 15). Primaries ten, nine, eight, and seven are very wide and, therefore, do not separate. This, obviously, increases turbulence and drag but provides low wing loading based upon the large wing area in relation to the weight of the bird. This condition enables the owl to fly slowly without stalling. Because the Barn Owl is largely nonmigratory, long, sustained flight capabilities are less important to the owl than is low wing loading, which makes it possible for the bird to survey a field more or less slowly and also to pick up a comparatively large item of prey. Barn Owls can hover for as long as one minute.

All of the primaries in the Barn Owl, since they overlap and never separate, do not need to be supplied with the fimbriae to reduce sound during flight. Primary number ten is the only one of the set that is provided with fimbriae, since this feather alone forms the leading

FIGURE 14. Emarginate wing tip of a Caspian Tern *(Sterna caspia),* typical of birds with high wing load.

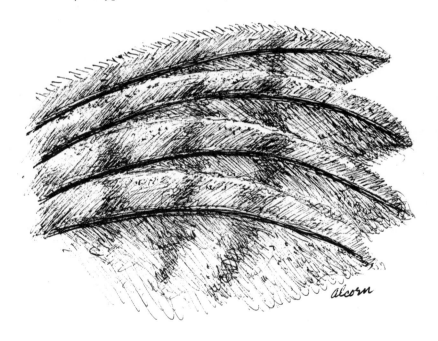

FIGURE 15. Truncate wing tip of Barn Owl, commonly found in birds with low wing load.

edge of the wing in flight. However, the dorsal surfaces of the other primaries are covered with a soft layer formed of the hairlike tips of the barbules (Figure 16). This velvety layer no doubt mutes the sound made by airflow over the top of the wing during flight. On the leading edge of the tenth primary, the barbs stand out separately and are recurved more or less like the teeth in a comb (Figure 17). Because of the nature of the wings, the flight of the Barn Owl is slow but buoyant and quiet.

In addition to small mammals, the food of the Barn Owl consists of birds, insects, frogs, and fish, in about

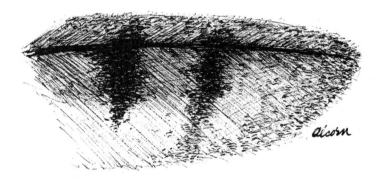

FIGURE 16. Barbules on the velvety dorsal surface of the Barn Owl wing.

FIGURE 17. Fimbriae of Barn Owl from the tenth primary.

that order of preference. Where prey species are not overly plentiful, a pair of Barn Owls may need as many as 70 acres in their hunting territory to adequately feed the young in the nest. When both parents are busy feeding a nestful of young and prey species are plentiful, as many as twenty mice per hour may be delivered.

The Barn Owl will nest in hollow trees, cliff ledges, holes in banks, deserted buildings, barns, towers, and belfries. Barn Owls can live compatibly with human civilization. Davie (1889), in his *Nests and Eggs of North American Birds,* listed the Barn Owl as a "constant resident of southern portions of the United States." In some areas in America, the spread of Barn Owl populations can be loosely correlated with the increase and spread of human communities into the countryside. As a rather striking example, in the Pacific Northwest forty and more years ago the Barn Owl was listed in Dawson and Bowles' (1909) hypothetical list as "presumptive" in the state of Washington. Kitchin (1932) listed the Barn Owl as rare in Washington. Jewett and others (1953) listed the Barn Owl in Washington as "an uncommon resident at moderate altitudes along the coast." The American Ornithologists' Union *Check List* of 1910 said of this species that it appeared "casually north to Oregon." Gabrielson (1959), in his *Birds of Alaska,* did not note the bird in that state, while Gabrielson and Jewett (1940), in *Birds of Oregon,* listed the Barn Owl as an "uncommon permanent resident in Oregon." While the species is not now commonly found north of the southern border of the western provinces of Canada, the Barn Owl is now commonly found throughout Washington, Idaho, and Oregon and restricts its nest sites almost entirely to man-made structures. Welty (1982) attributes the spread of the Barn Owl through New York state to the adoption of mechanical refrigeration and the abandonment of ice houses. Cer-

FIGURE 18. American Barn Owl.

tainly the Barn Owl is the owl most closely associated with humans. Barn Owls will use the same general area for nesting and also the same site for many generations. An old school belfry we visited a few years ago had refuse and pellets ankle-deep over the entire floor. It was possible to remove from this site literally thousands of these pellets. Sampling showed that over 95 percent of them contained the bones of field mice from the vicinity of the nesting area. Since superstitions have been built around owls, they have come to be thought of as birds of ill omen, misfortune, and death. The Barn Owl, because of its habit of associating its nesting area with dwellings, might be blamed for many reports of haunted houses.

The attrition rate is surprisingly high in Barn Owls, especially considering the fact that many have a protected site in barn or belfry. Barn rats seem not to be a threat to take the owlets for food. The practice of immediate incubation, when there are a number of days between egg depositions, would account for antagonistic pressures within the community. There may be loss of eggs during incubation, or starvation of young or weaker owlets in the nest. Eggs may be rolled off the nest, and young may freeze, starve, or fall to the ground due to the activities of all the birds in the nest. Nest attrition can also be correlated with depletion of prey species and inclemency of weather. In Barn Owls, broods of more than three or four rarely fledge and leave the nest when ready to fly. Barn Owls, being highly altricial, have little protection from the cold in the first weeks of nest life except for that provided by the parents and older nestmates. The young, naked at hatching, soon acquire their down cover, but supplemental heat must be provided for the nestling. At about three weeks, the face mask begins to appear in Barn Owls (Figure 20). After about one month, quill feathers make their appearance on the

FIGURE 19. Eggs of the Barn Owl.

FIGURE 20. Downy young of Barn Owl, about two weeks old. Note the early appearance of the face mask.

wings. Most young Barn Owls can fly at about the age of two months, although mature flight skills do not come until some weeks later.

Incubation in Barn Owls is largely a function of the female; the male bird does not develop a brood patch, although the male may attempt to incubate if the female is absent. If she is present, the male is pushed away. The eggs of the Barn Owl measure 42 to 49 mm by 31 to 36 mm and tend to be more oval than those of most other owls, white, not shiny or chalky. No nest is constructed, but eggs are placed on a ledge, rafter, or floor of attic or belfry. Since Barn Owls tend to use the same location year after year, old, dry pellets serve as a cushion for the eggs. Of interest is a data blank of a set of Barn Owl eggs collected in California on March 5, 1881. Several items on the blank are noteworthy:

> "*position* . . . Hole in bank of a deep barancha *ravine*. A bank about perpendicular and 25 ft. high; hole 5 ft. from

top and extending inward about 3 ft. nearly horizontally. Both owls driven from nest. Condition of eggs—as fresh as a full set can be gotten. Embryo not at all developed in 1, 2, 3."

One egg in the above set measured 49 mm by 36 mm, about 6 mm larger than the other seven eggs.

Immediate incubation means a great difference in the size of sibling owlets throughout the nest cycle, especially when the clutch size reaches eight eggs (rarely, one or two more). The incubation period is about one month—perhaps a day or two longer in northern latitudes. In areas where the climate is favorable, the Barn Owl may raise two broods a year. The life span of wild Barn Owls is approximately two to three years.

TYPICAL OWLS

The Typical Owl family consists of about 125 widely distributed species. The largest species reach a length of almost 30 inches, while the small ones are a little less than 6 inches. The plumage of the Typical Owl, as in all owls, is soft and long. These owls also show a variety of colors and patterns: brown, chestnut, gray or almost black, barred or streaked. In some (Screech Owl, Pygmy Owl, Flammulated Owl), the colors and patterns show mimicry as an aid to concealing coloration. In many, the tail is highly barred, and in others, there are plumicorns, sometimes called *ear tufts*. Some (Screech Owl) have color phases. As in all owls, the legs and toes are feathered, some completely and a few sparsely. Four toes are developed on each foot. The outer one of each is versatile in that it can be oriented forward or backward. This characteristic is used by the bird to attain greater security when perching. The eyes are large and are directed forward, and the sense of sight is well developed. There is a face mask or disc on the large head, and the neck is short. In the *Strigidae* the sense of hearing is acute, with the ear openings large and modified by a controlled fold of skin. In this family of owls the face disc serves, as it does in the Barn Owls, to aid the bird in pinpointing the origin of a sound. The wings are broad and rounded, and the nails are sharp and hooked. In most owls in this family, the female is usually somewhat larger than the male and perhaps more aggressive.

In the Typical Owl family only a few of the northern species are migratory. Migration in these is undoubtedly dictated by the climate and the decrease in available prey in the winter. Distribution is worldwide, except on some of the Pacific Ocean islands.

In habitat, Typical Owls are nocturnal or crepuscular, usually arboreal and usually solitary. The Burrowing Owl, the Short-eared Owl, and the Snowy Owl hunt by day. The nictitating membrane is used to protect the daylight hunters' eyes from the bright sunlight. Like that of the Barn Owl, the flight of the Typical Owl is noiseless and buoyant but not swift. While the fimbriae are limited to the tenth primary in the Barn Owl, they are found in many species of the *Strigidae* on the ninth and eighth, with vestiges showing on the sixth and seventh in a few. The principle food of this owl group consists of mammals, birds, reptiles, amphibians, insects, and fish. The members of the *Strigidae* are not skilled in constructing nests. Consequently, eggs are placed in the abandoned nests of other birds, the burrows of ground squirrels or prairie dogs (Burrowing Owl), in cavities in trees and other plants, in caves, on cliffsides, or on the ground. The eggs of most owls tend to be round; a few, however, are closer to an oval configuration. All eggs in the *Strigidae* are white and completely without pigment, but as incubation proceeds, the shells of some tend to be darker from staining by various materials in the nest. The average clutch size is four to seven eggs, mostly incubated by the female but sometimes helped by the male. The incubation period is about one month in most members of the *Strigidae*. In cold climates, it is not unusual for incubation to proceed for several days beyond the usual one month. In warmer climates, the incubation period may be as short as twenty-six days. This is commonly true for the Elf Owl in the dry areas of the southwest United States. Both sexes feed the young.

SCREECH OWL
Otus asio (Linnaeus)
Otus kennicottii (Elliot)

The first of the Typical Owls is the Screech Owl. The word *Otus* is Latin, meaning "Horned Owl." *Asio* is also Latin and seems to be synonymous with *Otus*, although it has been suggested that *asio* might be of Hebrew origin but with the meaning unknown. Carolus Linnaeus was a noted Swedish botanist, physician, and taxonomist born in May 1707 in Rashult, Province of Smaland, Sweden. He traveled extensively throughout Lapland and Upper Scandinavia. In one expedition in 1732 he traveled 4600 miles in upper Scandinavia and discovered 100 species of plants. A prolific writer, he authored 180 works, but he is probably best known as the father of the modern science of taxonomy based on characteristics, which led to the binary system of nomenclature that is used today. He died in 1778.

The species of the Western Screech Owl is named for Robert Kennicott, American naturalist and explorer, who was born in New Orleans in 1835 and died in Alaska in 1866. He contributed specimens to the Smithsonian and other institutions. Daniel Giraud Elliot was an American zoologist, who was born in 1831, died in 1915. He was a world traveler and contributor to many collections.

Screech Owls are small birds, measuring only 20 to 22 cm (8 to 9 in.). The owl is a resident in North America from Alaska across Canada and from lower California across the United States to Florida. Throughout the American range of the Screech Owl, two species are recognized, with a number of races. This owl is largely nonmigratory. The eastern American form (*O. asio*) may have a red phase in the plumage, alternating with the abundant gray of the ancestral color. The western species (*O. kennicottii*) may have a brown color phase alternating with a gray one, but the red phase does not occur here. In the Northwest the races of the Screech Owl tend to be darker than the other forms in America and do not usually alternate any color phases. In addition, the bill of the western form is much darker than that of the eastern species. The dividing line between the Eastern Screech Owl and the Western is approximately the Rocky Mountains. Both species are found in a variety of habitats, such as woodlands, parklands and adjacent brush borders, orchards, and open wooded lots. In the Northwest, the Screech Owl tends to favor habitats that are near water.

FIGURE 21. Screech Owl.

The Screech Owl will lay its eggs in an old wood-pecker hole or in a natural hollow in a tree. The nests are usually found in well-wooded localities bordering some open parkland. The nest may be placed as high as 60 feet off the ground or as low as 4 feet. Two to five eggs are laid, four being the average number. The eggs are typi-cally roundish and measure 36 to 41 mm by 31 to 33 mm.

Screech Owls tend to be strong, faithful incubators. In checking over old nest records of these species, I found such remarks as:

Bird had to be lifted from nest.

Bird had to be lifted from eggs.

Bird hardly moved as I took eggs from under her.

A cavity [nest] in a dead limb of a cottonwood tree....The limb had broken off just above the nest a day or so before the set was collected, but the female brooded on. The top of the nest was exposed after the accident.

FIGURE 22. Eggs of the Screech Owl.

The Screech Owl enjoys a great variety of food in its diet. A number of years ago, Bowles (see Dawson 1909) recorded the contents of the stomach of a Screech Owl, taken in January in freezing weather, containing cutworms, centipedes, crickets, beetles, and other insect remains. Bowles goes on to state that many years ago Dr. Shaver raised exotic game birds such as Ring-necked and Golden Pheasants at his summer home, now on Fort Lewis, Washington reserve land. One morning, Shaver noticed a number of dead birds that had been killed by "gnashes and rips" in the head and neck, which he blamed on rats. A few days later, a number of prize Bantam chickens were mangled and dead, in addition to valuable male golden pheasants. Since there was no indication of what killed the birds, Shaver deliberately sprinkled strychnine into the body cavity of one of the Bantams. The next morning he found the body of a dead Screech Owl with the claws of one foot imbedded in the body of the chicken. There are a number of records of the Screech Owl eating angleworms. According to Rathbun, in Bent (1938), a number of years ago he killed and skinned a Screech Owl to find in its stomach a solid packed mass of ants—the large, black pismires sometimes found so commonly about farm buildings. Screech Owls will eat crayfish with relish where these invertebrates are available.

In spite of the liberal population of Screech Owls in their various habitats, comparatively few nests are found. This may be in part because the bird is secretive—extremely so during the breeding season— and is unusually quiet. Indeed, the "screech" of this bird is rarely given. The lilting, tremulous voice is most often heard during the autumn months. In spring and summer the birds are quiet and almost mute. Also, it is difficult to see the Screech Owl, as it sits quietly in a tree next to the trunk in a perfect example of mimicry (Figure 23).

FIGURE 23. Western Screech Owl showing mimicry of the
bark of the tree.

A number of years ago I was camped on the shores of Ozette Lake, Washington with E.A. Kitchin. Kitch was one of the fine naturalists who developed much of our ornithology in the Northwest and who was always enthusiastic about getting into the field. It was about two o'clock in the morning, and we lay wrapped in sleeping bags on the grassy slopes of the lake. It was quiet, cool, and still, with a pale moon about half full and mists rising over the water. Kitch was not young and had fallen into the habit of waking at about two o'clock and, as he said, taking a "siesta" with a pipeful of tobacco. I suppose it was the aroma of the tobacco and the movements he made next to me that awoke me. We stretched out in the sleeping bags and discussed the beauties of the scene and bird life in general. From a spruce tree over our heads came the bell-like, musical song of a friendly Screech Owl. There is nothing quite like the call of this bird in a wild setting. I suspect it was curiosity (not the aroma of the tobacco) that brought the bird to us, and as Kitch lay puffing his pipe and the tobacco glowed with every puff, the little owl would dive-bomb the pipe. Maybe it was the sight of the glowing coals, or maybe it was just us. At any rate, this performance went on for some time. Kitch would take the pipe and place it at arm's length on a convenient rock, at which time the owl would pay no attention to it. But when Kitch clamped the stem between his teeth and brought the coals to life, the owl would visit us again by way of the dive-bomb. I cannot imagine any bird as astute as this owl mistaking those glowing embers for something to eat. It had to be curiosity and the bird's investigative spirit that stimulated this behavior.

WHISKERED SCREECH OWL

Otus trichopsis (Wagler)

Trichopsis is the Greek for "hairy appearance." This is an allusion to the stiff, bristly feathers surrounding the bird's bill and the face mask. Wagler did most of his work in Mexico and named this owl in 1832. This species is also sometimes called the Spotted Screech Owl. The range of the species covers the region from the mountains of southern Arizona south through Mexico to Guatemala and Honduras. In habitat it prefers the white oak associations in the mountains between 4900 and 6500 feet altitude. There is some overlap with the Western Screech Owl. Identification in the field is sometimes made by the voice of this owl, and it is generally found higher in elevation than the Western. There is little, if any, overlap with the Eastern Screech Owl. There is a distinct dichromatism in the Whiskered Screech Owl, since it has gray and red phases. But it is a comparatively little known species, perhaps because of the difficulty of observing and studying it in its native habitat.

In form, it is much like a Screech Owl, but it is distinctly smaller, averaging only 17 to 20 cm (7 to 8 in.). The large white spots on the neck, the large black spots on the upper parts, and the feathers of the upper wing coverts are the conspicuous markings of the species. However, a specimen in the hand labeled an adult male shows broad, dark bands on the undersurfaces and a lack of the typical white spots on the lower hind neck and on the wing coverts. In most all the other markings it is like a Screech Owl but decidedly smaller in size.

FIGURE 24.
Whiskered Screech Owl.

There are comparatively few authentic nesting records of the Whiskered Owl. This may be due in part to the elusive and secretive nature of the bird and in part to the difficulty of finding the nesting bird in the mountainous terrain that it inhabits. The records that are known show the bird using old woodpecker holes or a natural cavity in a tree for nesting. The eggs of the Whiskered Owl are similar to the eggs of the Screech Owl but are considerably smaller. The eggs of this species will average 34 to 40 mm by 30 to 32 mm and tend to be round.

The food of the Whiskered Screech Owl consists largely of the larvae and adults of insects and centipedes. The presence of certain ground-inhabiting insects in the stomachs of some specimens of this owl might indicate that, in part, this species may feed on the ground. The bird is seldom seen higher than 30 feet above the ground and usually much lower.

FLAMMULATED OWL

Otus flammeolus (Kaup)

The root of *flammeolus* is from the Latin meaning a bright, flaming red object. This alludes to the rusty brown color that streaks the back of this little owl, up over the wing coverts and around the face disc. Kaup worked in Mexico and first named this owl in 1852. This bird is Saw-whet sized and is sometimes referred to as the Flammulated Screech Owl; but its color, its color pattern, and its size obviously put it outside of the Screech Owl category. In addition, unlike the Screech Owl, the little Flammulated species has dark, chocolate-brown eyes. (The Screech Owl has bright yellow eyes.)

The Flammulated Owl ranges from southern British Columbia to the highlands of Mexico and Guatemala. It is found as far east as Colorado, New Mexico, western Texas, and eastern sections of California and east of the mountain ranges in Oregon, Washington, and British Columbia. It is not a coastal bird in any of its range, and unlike many other owls, it is quite migratory, so that it winters chiefly south of the United States.

The Flammulated Owl is a dichromatic species, distinctly smaller than the Screech, measuring 15 to 17 cm (6 to 7 in.). The red phase seems to be present only in

FIGURE 25. Flammulated Owl.

the birds in their southern range. The body has transverse bands of grayish white. The upper breast and wing coverts and the area around the eye and around the ear openings are rusty rufous. The feathers immediately over the eyes are white, and there are small, rounded ear tufts. This mixture of color and the overall pattern of the bird make it possible for it to blend in with its surroundings. If it is sitting quietly next to the trunk of a tree, it is very inconspicuous.

Even though this species is probably quite widely distributed within its range, it is not well known. This may be due to the fact that it blends so well into its surroundings. It also tends to be solitary and shy. These facts, coupled with the difficulty of the terrain, probably account for the apparent rarity of this owl.

Like many others, the Flammulated Owl nests in old flicker holes and natural cavities in trees. It lays three or four pure white eggs that are somewhat smaller than the Screech Owl's eggs, measuring 28 to 30 mm by 24 to 25 mm. As in most owls, the eggs of this species are roundish. The food of this owl is largely insects. It may occasionally capture a small bird or a small mammal. Various stomachs when examined have been found to contain insects such as ants, caterpillars, crickets, beetles, grasshoppers, and related forms such as spiders and scorpions.

GREAT HORNED OWL

Bubo virginianus (Gmelin)

Bubo is the Latin for Horned Owl, and *virginianus* comes from the Latinization of "Virginia," where the first Horned Owl was described. Johann Friedrich Gmelin was a German physician born in Tubingen, August 1748. He spent an active career until his death, practicing medicine and working in natural history. He edited the thirteenth edition of *Systema Natura* of Linneaus during the years 1788 to 1793. He is the author of numerous publications on natural history. He died in Gottingen in 1804.

The Great Horned Owl and the Snowy Owl are the

largest of our owls, with the Great Horned measuring 52 to 58 cm (21 to 23 in.). It is a resident in the Americas from the Arctic to the Straits of Magellan, except that it is not found in the West Indies. There are about ten races of it within its range. These ten recognized races occupy every distinct habitat within that range. The Horned Owl is a bird of the forest, from the heavily wooded area along the northern border states to the less heavily wooded regions of Utah, New Mexico, Texas, and south into Mexico. Chiefly because it is so widely dispersed, racial forms show a great diversity in color—from the dark feathers found along the humid region of the Pacific coast of Alaska, British Columbia, Washington, and Oregon to the pale types that occupy the semiarid regions in southeastern California, Nevada, and Southern Utah. The change in color is so striking in Horned Owls that at one time a race known as the Arctic Horned Owl occupied the area from southern Canada north. Whether the overall light plumage was caused by selectivity due to the white Arctic environment or simply a natural reaction to an interior distribution has never been agreed upon by ornithologists. Since there tends to be some considerable movement north and south in the northern populations, such colors may be simply due to natural variations and should not constitute definite races. There are a number of examples to show that the so-called white, northern race does come south into the northern tier of states. While the plumage of the Great Horned Owls differs greatly in individuals, all show a mixture of brown and varying shades of black and buff, with a considerable number of feathers showing white, especially under the chin. The eyes are large, the beak and claws are sharp, and there is a complete, soft covering of feathers over the toes down to the base of the nails. Two large plumicorns are developed and are very obvious.

FIGURE 26. Great Horned Owl.

Seton (1890) described the Horned Owl very well when he said:

> Their untameable ferocity . . . Their magnificent bearing; their objection to carrion and strictly carnivorous taste—would make me rank these winged tigers amongst the most pronounced and savage birds of prey.

This owl is also known for its variety of voices, variously called shrieks, hoots, barks, growls, and blood-curdling screams. This large vocabulary is colorfully set forth by Dawson (1909) in the quaint (and florid!) language of the time, describing the vocal behavior of the Great Horned Owl. As a young man, the writer once lived

> immediately adjoining a large wooden church building. The chamber window looked upon a flat kitchen roof thru which projected a brick chimney some ten feet away. At three o'clock one morning a horrible nightmare gave way to a still more horrible waking. Murder most foul was being committed on the roof just outside the open window, and the shrieks of the victims (at least seven of them!) were drowned by the imprecations of the attacking party—fire-eating pirates to the number of a dozen. Pandemonium reigned and my bones were liquid with fright—when suddenly the tumult ceased; nor could I imagine thru a whole sick day what had been the occasion of the terrifying visitation. But two weeks later the conflict was renewed, at a merciful distance this time. Peering out into the moonlight I beheld one of these Owls perched upon the chimney of the church hard by, gibbering and shrieking like one possessed. Cat-calls, groans, and demoniacal [sic] laughter were varied by wails and screeches, as of souls in torment—an occasion most memorable. The previous serenade had evidently been rendered from the kitchen chimney, and I pray never to hear its equal.

The carnivorous diet and the savagery of the Great Horned Owl has not made it very popular with sportsmen, the farmer, and the breeder of game birds. In fairly recent years, there has been a marked difference in the attitude of ornithologists toward the role that raptors should play in the biological economy and the preservation of bird species highly valued by humans. Bowles (1917) says that in the winter of 1916 the Horned Owls "became so numerous as to be a veritable pest. Poultry farms of all kinds were raided without mercy." At one game farm, captive wild ducks numbering fifty-three were quickly reduced to twenty-six, taken by Horned Owls. Many of the owls were shot, but most were killed by poison placed in the uneaten carcasses. On Vancouver Island in the same year, out of a "plague of Horned Owls," hundreds were shot. Many stomachs were opened and contained, in addition to ducks, chickens, captive pheasants, grouse, and Canada geese. In these modern times, while we still recognize the ferocity of the Horned Owl, we now regard it as a valuable segment of our avifauna, and have no thought of mechanical or artificial methods or techniques to manage raptor populations.

The Great Horned Owl feeds upon all manner of birds and mammals, from birds the size of meadowlarks up to and including small geese. The versatility of the Great Horned Owl's diet intrigued the correspondents of more than a century ago. In the May 1882 *Forest and Stream* (Bendire 1892), a writer states that a Great Horned Owl's nest contained two young owls and

> a mouse, a young muskrat, two eels, four bullheads, a Woodcock, four Ruffed Grouse, one rabbit, and eleven rats. The food taken out of the nest weighed almost eighteen pounds. A curious fact connected with these captives was that the heads were eaten off, the bodies being untouched.

There are many examples of the owl feeding on chickens, ducks, and lesser Canada geese—all birds that are larger and heavier than the owl itself. The owl also will feed upon many types of mammals, from small rodents up to and including the house cat. It has long been known that the Horned Owl will feed on skunk, as many early references to the food habits of the Big Horned Owl noted that the skunk was popular with this species. Samuels (1872) made a direct reference to the propensity of the owl to eat skunk:

> Rabbits, grouse, and other birds fall victims to his rapacity; and I have often shot individuals of this species, whose feathers were so impregnated with the peculiar odor of the skunk as to be unbearable at a near approach.

In the farming country of British Columbia, the Horned Owl is particularly disliked by the farmer because the house cat, kept to aid in decreasing the population of mice and rats around the barn, is commonly picked up by the owl. The cat may be big enough that the owl may be able to carry it away only with difficulty, but in most instances the cat is eaten upon the ground. The Horned Owl will tackle a porcupine and will often feed upon skunk with considerable relish. Apparently, the odor from the skunk does not make the meat any less palatable. I recall in some high school and college years working in the shop of a commercial taxidermist. I will never forget the feeling of excitement when I handled, for the first time, a Great Horned Owl with its soft feathers, bright eyes, and long, sharp talons. During the years in that occupation, I had the opportunity and "privilege" of skinning and preparing mounted birds for the sportsmen who wanted trophies for their dens. It was a rare Horned Owl received in the taxidermy shop that did not possess the odor of skunk. It became necessary to spray the bird with a deodorant substance to make it possible for mere humans to take care of the preparation.

It was my practice always to examine the stomach of each owl specimen, simply out of curiosity. There were many mammals, including rabbits, birds, and saltwater ducks, that had fallen prey to the owl. I once kept a captive Horned Owl in a rather spacious den adjacent to (but screened from!) the chicken yard on the farm where I lived. I could enter the pen but had to do so with a hat on my head and a heavy coat covering my arms. I learned that I had little to fear from the snapping beak of the bird, but I had better stay away from the claws; the hiss was all bluff. I fed him a pigeon a day that I had live-trapped near the taxidermy shop. I could sacrifice the pigeon before tossing it into the pen, or I could put it into the pen alive; it made no difference to the owl. When he finally came to tolerate me, he always relished the pigeon without an antagonistic display toward me. After a period of several years, he began to show signs of age, and finally, out of compassion, I dispatched him, feeling that he might not be able to make it by himself in the wild. He now occupies an honored place among our museum skins.

The Horned Owl is a bird of the trees, so its nests are found off the ground. It will use an old hawk nest or the bulky nest of some other tree dweller. There are even records of Horned Owls occupying the old nest of the blue heron. They also seek out a natural cavity in a tree or build their own scanty nest in a fork of a large tree. In the southwest part of the United States and in eastern Washington state, where the trees may be small or scarce, the Horned Owl will take to a rock ridge or even a hole in a bank. The nest can be a few feet off the ground, or it can be high in a tree or cliffside. The clutch commonly contains three or four roundish eggs that measure 52 to 56 mm by 44 to 48 mm.

The entire nesting process of this owl has long intrigued naturalists and ornithologists. Nest building and egg laying begin early in the season. In the Puget Sound Museum is a set of Horned Owl eggs collected in Florida on the sixteenth of December. The late Don Nicholson noted on the data with the set of eggs, "not uncommon to lay in December." The Horned Owl, throughout its range and even in the northern states, will have fresh eggs in the process of being incubated throughout the months of February and March. In the northland there may be considerable snow, frost, and ice while a complete new clutch of eggs is being incubated.

It has long been a source of wonderment why the Horned Owl must start its egg laying so early in the season, even in the cold northland. It is probably necessary to start the procedures early because of the unique characteristics of the entire breeding season of the Horned Owl. Incubation periods last for about thirty days. The young do not open their eyes for perhaps as long as ten days after hatching. After the eyes are open, brooding continues for a period of about four weeks. At this age in the Horned Owl, the dark down is a warmer dress than the original white and is undoubtedly an adaption in deference to the cold of the early season. They may leave the nest only after they are four or five weeks old, and they do not fly until they are about ten weeks old. During the nesting period and before they fly, they are well fed and protected by the parents. Even beyond this, the young birds commonly follow the parents for many weeks, crying for the food that is still provided to them by the parents. It is not uncommon for families of owls to stay together and share food for periods of up to a year, and it is probably very common

FIGURE 27. Eggs of the Great Horned Owl.

practice for a family to stay together until the young, in turn, start their own breeding cycles at about one year of age.

I recall with great pleasure a week in late March several years ago that I spent in the north-central area of the province of British Columbia. The lakes were still solidly frozen; the ground was hard; a few inches of snow covered everything; the nights were quiet and cold. It was a wild country, and on still, dark nights it was inspiring to hear the hooting of the owls as they called and answered each other in that cold northland. Their songs traveled and echoed back and forth throughout the silence of the night. When daylight arrived, their voices ceased while the business of eating, resting, and incubating continued. It took some time to find a nesting

FIGURE 28.
Downy young of Great
Horned Owl, several
days old.

female on a set of eggs. The discovery came when we noted some pellets and bones around the base of a large tree. It is incredible (and obviously this was circumstantial evidence) that an owl could dispatch and eat a beaver, but there were, nonetheless, several beaver skulls picked clean of meat among the bones at the base of that tree. As I walked around the tree, the female, sitting on her eggs, watched me carefully, only her head showing above the crest of the nest. She was alarmed and disturbed, and with her ear tufts alternately fully erect and flattened out and her large yellow eyes following my movements, she presented quite a picture. The farmer who accompanied me felt it his duty to kill the bird because of the damage her kind cause to his chickens. When the deed was done and I had the limp form in my hand, I noticed the unusally large bare area. This is a bare area of skin, called a brood patch. It stretches from the upper breast to the lower abdomen. The feathers from the nest had obviously come from this part of the brooding female. The brood patch was hot and soft from the lymph fluid that had developed just under the surface of the skin. Since the nights and the days were cold, this warm brood area of the mother owl had to be in direct contact with the eggs to keep them from chilling or, indeed, freezing.

SNOWY OWL
Nyctea scandiaca (Linnaeus)

The Snowy Owl derives its name from the Greek *nycteus,* meaning "nocturnal." The species *scandiaca* is the Latinization of "Scandinavia." The type specimen of the Snowy Owl was originally discovered in the Scandinavian countries of Europe.

   The Snowy Owl is a large—50 to 61 cm (20 to 24 in.)—and powerful bird and has a wide distribution throughout the arctic regions of the world. It breeds on the arctic tundra north of the major tree lines in the Northern Hemisphere. It is widely, but not necessarily evenly, distributed, since much of its population density depends on the distribution of its food. The major article of its diet is the lemming, but it will accept other mammals, birds, fish, and, if necessary, carrion. There are records dating back as far as 1882 pointing out the population densities of the Snowy Owl in relation to the lemming densities. If there are abundant lemmings, there are usually large populations of the owl; and in winter, when the lemming populations drop, the owl moves south to look for sufficient food. In consequence, there are many winters when large numbers of Snowy Owls come down across the Canadian border to the northern tier of the United States. Snowy Owls have been seen as far south as Utah in the west and through the state of North Carolina along the Atlantic coast. In the autumn of 1843, two Snowy Owls were shot at Bass Cove in Bermuda. There are casual records in Louisiana, Kentucky, and West Virginia. One early Kentucky specimen was taken in the year 1810. Since the Snowy Owl is an inhabitant of the tundra, it spends much of its life on the ground. In the wintertime, however, when it comes south into civilization, it is not uncommon to see it perched on a convenient power pole, a fence post, or even high on a building in a city. In its native habitat in the north, it spends much of its time sitting on a hummock so that it can survey the adjacent tundra to look for movement in the moss and lichens which might indicate lemming. The bird may sit for hours, completely motionless but alert, listening and watching for any sound or slight movement. While such a bird, with its white pattern, does not blend in with its surroundings, the unwary prey item will give its presence away by its slightest movement.

The female tends to be somewhat larger than the male, a condition not uncommon among predators. The Snowy Owl is not completely white. Most of the body

FIGURE 29. Snowy Owl.

feathers of the female are liberally barred with dark brown or black. The male has fewer bars, which are more widely spaced and narrower. The black markings go up over the back of the head in the female, while the head of the male tends to be more snow-white. In both sexes, the throat and chin are white. The darker female, who does most of the incubation, may be rendered less conspicuous against the tundra background because of her darker feathers. A small adult breeding male, with his plumage of an immaculate white, is a startlingly beautiful bird, unbelievable and unreal in flight. Young students of ornithology find it difficult to reconcile the beauty of form, color, and feather pattern with the ferocity and bold determination evident in the Snowy Owl. Perhaps the severity of the environment in which the owl dives, hunts, and dies dictates, through natural selection, the fierce disposition found in this extraordinarily beautiful creature.

The Snowy Owl is completely at home in the tundra, but when it appears in wintertime around the bays and open spaces away from its native habitat, it suffers from a lack of knowledge or instinct to survive well in the different type of habitat. So the Snowy Owl finds some difficulty in acquiring sufficient food to keep it in good health when it visits south of its natural range. Since the native northern lemming is not present for the owl visitors, the bird turns to a different type of food, and not always successfully. It does not seem to live well on the native populations of field mice or other small rodents. Consequently, the southern owl visitor turns to a bird diet, perhaps because these are more visible and easier to catch. Many owls that find themselves around the dunes and fields adjacent to waterfowl often pick up crippled ducks injured by the shotgun of the duck hunter. A few years ago, I prepared a specimen of a Snowy Owl whose stomach contained a complete Green-winged Teal. Contained in the body of the Teal were a number of lead pellets from a shotgun blast. As a result of the change to a less rich diet, the Snowy Owls decline, and as they become subject to owl diseases, they become debilitated and weakened. There is also a marked increase in the number of ectoparasites plaguing the owls when their resistance drops. There is evidence that most of the Snowy Owls that visit the south in the wintertime do not ever return to the tundra. It may be that in their weakened condition they are not able to make the flight, or it may be that their instinct for migration, and therefore their sense of direction, is not well enough developed to find and make their way back to the Arctic. It may be, too, that they do not recognize suitable habitats along the flyway to feed and thereby recover their strength. It is a common sight in the wintertime around the southern dunes and fields to find Snowy Owls so weakened that some can be picked up by hand. This diminished strength may be another reason why many of the owls have been shot by duck hunters during the winter.

The Snowy Owl rivals the Great Horned Owl in ferocity, vigor, and skill in hunting its prey. It is a strong and silent flyer and has an acute sense of hearing and excellent eyesight. It is likewise largely diurnal, in spite of the Greek meaning of the genus. The Snowy Owl, in addition to its favorite lemming on the tundra, will eat ground squirrels, rabbits, and birds. The ptarmigan is a favorite in its diet, probably partly because the ptarmigan is easy to catch. Dufresne (1922), quoted in Bent (1938), said:

> I estimate carefully and with no wish to exaggerate that a single snowy owl will destroy three hundred game birds in a year. The average conception among the hunters is that it is twice that many, and they may be right. I, myself, have seen one bird kill three full grown ptarmigan within an hour.

When the adult owl is feeding its young, many newly hatched ptarmigan are fed to the young owls, perhaps because the ptarmigan chicks have soft bones, making digestion easier and regurgitation of pellets less necessary in the nestling owls. An example of the Snowy Owl's skill was described by Nelson (1887), who watched one catch a large arctic hare. The owl put one foot in the hare's back and stretched out the other foot, dragging it like a brake on the snow and ground. When the hare stopped struggling because of exhaustion, it was neatly and quickly killed by the bird. The "character" of the Snowy Owl is well illustrated by Brewster (1925), quoted in Bent (1938), in an incident about the year 1850:

> According to my notes, a man named Abbott, living not far from the post office on Upton Hill, surprised a Snowy Owl in the act of killing a hen *directly under his barn*, and dispatched it with a club, for instead of attempting to escape, it faced him boldly, and refused to relinquish its prize. It must have been hard pressed by hunger to behave this rashly.

Dufresne's approach to the Snowy Owl problem is reflected in his statement:

> As soon as the young ptarmigan hatched my observations of the snowy owl became a record of slaughter. I had no way of telling exactly how many were eaten on account of the softness of the bones, but I do know that rodent regurgitation practically ceased at this time. Ptarmigan, both old and young, became the mainstay of the seven pairs of owls and their combined families which I had under observation. I destroyed six of the nests, procuring both old birds in each instance, but I decided to watch the seventh nest to the bitter end, hoping to see a reversion to the rodent diet, but it was useless.

This is another example of an opinion (discussed briefly in the Great Horned Owl section) held by naturalists of a former day, who regarded predation as an evil if prey species were, in the eyes of humans, more valuable than the raptor.

The nest of the Snowy Owl is scooped out of the lichens on a dry hummock. The bird will lay an average of three or four eggs, but five to seven are not uncommon. The eggs measure approximately 45 to 47 mm by 57 to 61 mm. The color is pure white, with the egg

FIGURE 30. Eggs of the Snowy Owl.

tending to be more elongated than the usual roundish shape of most owl eggs. The young hatch in about one month. Since the adult begins to incubate as soon as the first egg is laid, and there may be a couple of days between laying, the young birds hatch in intervals. There is, therefore, a distinct advantage given to the older nestling. The first hatched owl in a nest may be as much as two weeks older than the last to hatch.

The dark down color is especially useful in the cold to keep the young warmer. The first adult plumage appears at the end of the summer before the cold weather of the north sets in. The whitest birds are males, and the females tend to be more heavily barred. The female takes care of the incubation. The male feeds her as she incubates and, in addition, will defend the nest.

NORTHERN HAWK OWL
Surnia ulula (Linnaeus)

Linnaeus originally described the Hawk Owl and named it *Strix ulula*. The genus *Surnia* was applied to this species in the year 1806. While the derivation of the word Surnia is unknown, *ulula* is a Latin term for "owl" and probably was originally given to this bird because of an onomatopoeic comparison. Actually, the species *ulula* is an early Plinian name given to the Screech Owl. Coues (1874) translated the Greek *ululo* as meaning "I howl," "halloo," or making a "hullabaloo."

The Hawk Owl is circumboreal in distribution, inhabiting the forests of northern Scandinavia, Russia, Siberia, Alaska, Canada, south in North America to northern Washington, central Alberta, the northern tier of the United States, and the southern part of the eastern provinces of Canada. While the Hawk Owl in North America is not highly migratory, there are records of it as far south as Nebraska, Illinois, northern Ohio, and New Jersey. It is a bird of the forest.

Hawk Owls have a long tail and a hawklike flight, which accounts for the common name of the bird. The eyes are relatively small, but the iris is a clear, luminous yellow like that of most other owls. It has a small facial disc, not as prominent as in other owls, and lacks ear tufts. But it gives the impression of a compact, sleek appearance and does not have the fluffy feathers that are so characteristic of most owls, especially the larger ones. Hawk Owls like to hunt from the tree tops and are active in the evening during the hours of dusk but often also during the day. The Hawk Owl is probably the most diurnal of all the owls, along with the Short-eared, Burrowing, and Pygmy Owls. The ear openings are not as large as they are in many of the other owls and do not have a movable cover. These characteristics may account, in part, for this diurnal behavior. It flies over the woods, tundra, and parkland of the north in an erratic fashion similar to that of a small hawk. The owl, being of medium size and with its long, wedge-shaped, pointed tail, is frequently mistaken for a hawk or falcon. This species measures approximately 35 to 40 cm (14 to 16 in.).

When the eggs are hard-set or there are young still in the nest, Hawk Owls become very aggressive. Grinnell (1900) described an encounter he had with an incubating pair of Hawk Owls in northern Alaska. The male flew at Grinnell and struck him full weight on the skull, drawing blood from claw marks on his scalp. His hat, he says, "was torn and thrown twelve feet."

The Hawk Owl usually lays three to seven eggs, seven being quite common, but on occasion, there may be as many as nine. The eggs are pure white, round, smooth, and somewhat glossy, and measure 30 to 32 mm by 39 to 40 mm. The incubation begins as soon as the first egg is laid and lasts about one month. The young, therefore, hatch on a staggered schedule. The eggs are deposited in an old flicker or woodpecker hole, on occasions in the natural hole of a dead tree. The owls will often find a cavity in which there are mosses and grasses that have probably been placed there by squirrels, since the owl usually lays the eggs directly on wood chips. Often the nest floor will contain the bones of prey items picked clean (Figure 31). These bones have obviously never been swallowed and ejected in the form of pellets. The assumption is made that the soft parts of the prey are eaten by the brooding parent. There is a possibility that the bones have been picked clean by a previous brood, but the former assumption may appear to be a little more credible. The female bird will pull the feathers from her breast, flanks, and abdomen and sometimes from the inside of her legs to help preserve warmth around the developing eggs. The brood patch thus developed and exposed is thick and soft and warm. While I have never observed a fresh brood patch on an incubating Hawk Owl, I have seen it on a number of other owls. If it is pressed with the fingers, lymph fluid may ooze from the surface of the skin. It is almost turgid. The Hawk Owl has one of the largest and most efficient brood patches of all the owls. This is one of nature's mechanisms to aid in retaining warmth for the incubating egg and the young, since the nesting area is in the northland at times when frost and snow are still common.

The white down of the young changes to a cinnamon brown in a few weeks. This is the pattern of most owls, but it seems to be much more obvious in those birds that habitually live and nest in the tundra country

FIGURE 31. Eggs of the Hawk Owl.

or in the cold of the north. This is probably very necessary in owls, since, being so highly altricial, they are
vulnerable to the cold during their long residency in the
nest.

The food of the Hawk Owl consists largely of mice,
lemmings, weasels and other small ground mammals,
and occasionally fish. In the wintertime, when the mam-
malian population drops or it becomes otherwise difficult to find sufficient mammals, the Hawk Owl will turn
to the ptarmigan for its staple article of diet. It will feed
on small birds and insects when these become available.
It has been stated that the Hawk Owl is capable of killing
and carrying off a ruffed grouse. There is some doubt,
however, as to the accuracy of this statement, as it is
questionable whether the wing load of a Hawk Owl
could accommodate the weight of a grouse.

Brewster (1885) noted a memorable flight of Hawk
Owls in New England in 1884. Here, incidentally, is another instance of the change in attitude from a century
ago concerning the value or harm of the raptor. In that
year

> a flight of Hawk Owls was unparalleled in any previous
> year of which we have definite records . . . so that a
> single taxidermist in Bangor, Maine (Mr. Bowler) received
> no less than twenty-eight freshly killed specimens in the
> course of a few weeks . . . . These figures doubtless
> represent but a small proportion of the total number
> killed, for in the region over which the birds spread, few
> persons are aware that an Owl has any commerical value,
> although everyone shoots the despised bird at sight.
> Thus for every one preserved a dozen were thrown away.
> As instancing this, I quote the following from a short
> note in 'Forest and Stream', signed Ned Norton, and

dated at Colebrooke, N.H., Dec. 1:— Hawk Owls came three weeks ago in greater numbers than ever seen before. Farmers' sons have been killing them all over the country.

NORTHERN PYGMY OWL
Glaucidium gnoma (Wagler)

Coues (1874) finds it difficult to reconcile himself to the generic term *Glaucidium*. This term supposedly arises from the word *glaucous*, used to denote something that is bluish. No owl has blue eyes, but Homer refers to Minerva as the "blue-eyed" goddess. Therefore, since the owl is the bird of wisdom and was held sacred by Minerva, the reference may be strictly to the goddess and have no relationship to the color of the bird's eye. But there is also a relationship between the species *gnoma* and Minerva. This term is derived from the Greek for "reason," "decision," and "opinion" (all from the

87

original Greek meaning "I know"). We see this derivation carried a little farther in English words from the root
gnostic. Again, since Minerva is the goddess of wisdom,
it is appropriate that *gnoma* be applied to the owl.

The Pygmy Owl is strictly western in distribution. It
is found from southeastern Alaska through the Rocky
Mountains to Baja California and as far south as Guatemala. It is a resident bird throughout all of its range.
There are related species within the genus in other parts
of the world. *Glaucidium passerinum* is found in a belt
from Central Europe and Scandinavia through central
Asia and east to the Pacific coast. The Ferruginous Owl,
sometimes called the Ferruginous Pygmy Owl *(Glaucidium brasilianum)* (discussed next), is found from Mexico,
Arizona, and Texas through South America to the southern part of that continent. The Northern Pygmy Owl is
usually found in North America at higher elevations
than *G. brasilianum,* but along the coast at sea level and
in the rain forest the northern species is a common bird.
The Least Pygmy Owl *(Glaucidium minutissimum)* is found
from Mexico to southern Brazil. The Pygmy is a forest
species, frequenting the glades and brush borders of
open fields adjacent to the trees.

The Pygmy Owl measures 15 to 16 cm (6 to 6½ in.).
The back, crown, and tail are suffused with a rich ochre
brown, heavily dotted with small, light spots. The
"perky" tail is long and has white interrupted bars. Dark
brown stripes predominate on the under side. The
Pygmy Owl is one of the few that exhibits mimicry. The
two black nape spots outlined by white appear to be eyes
(Figure 33). Strangely enough, this characteristic is never
mentioned in the older literature but was recognized by
the "amateur" ornithologist of sixty years ago. Charles
W. Michael, while watching the Pygmy Owl one day,
wrote to Bent (1938):

FIGURE 32. Northern Pygmy Owl.

FIGURE 33.
A case of mimicry;
"false eyes" in the Northern Pygmy Owl.

With a lightning movement he would turn his head half-
way around, presenting the back of his head to us. And
as we watched this wonderful head, which appeared at
times to turn completely about, we got the impression
that the owl was double faced; for when he turned away
his face we saw a second face on the back of his head—a
white beak and closed eyes under beetling brows. Close
scrutiny showed this beak to be a white feather and the
eyebrows and eyes produced by an arrangement of feathers. Nevertheless, this make-believe face was a very good
one, and we wondered if nature had bestowed this second face upon the little owl to fool his enemies. With two
faces the pygmy owl can really look one way while appearing to look the other way. Neither his enemies nor
his potential victims can be sure just which way he is
looking, all of which is to the advantage of the bloodthirsty little demon. He is like the teacher who hides his
eyes behind dark glasses—the scholars can never tell just
which way those eyes are looking.

The Pygmy Owl nests, as many other owls do, in the cavity of an old woodpecker hole or in a natural cavity in a dead tree. It lays three to six eggs with an average clutch of five. The eggs, as those of other owls, are roundish and pure white. They measure 28 to 32 mm by 23 to 25 mm. They are placed in the nest cavity without any nest material except some scattered bones and feathers of birds that were eaten if the nest was previously

FIGURE 34. Eggs of the Northern Pygmy Owl.

occupied by an owl. Generally, this nest is placed adjacent to a field or meadow. The nest is probably placed in accordance with the owl's food preferences, which consist largely of mice and insects that are to be found in the open fields. The Pygmy Owl, however, is not above taking other types of food. It will, if available, pick up lizards and other reptiles, and it will often take sparrows, juncos, and small birds that are found along the borders of the habitat. It has been noted often that a field adjacent to the nesting hole of a Pygmy Owl family will often be devoid of small bird life.

During its breeding season, the Pygmy Owl can become quite diurnal. At other times of the year, it is crepuscular but not as nocturnal as many other owls. Like other owls, it exhibits a considerable degree of curiosity. It is not unusual or difficult for a person to lure the Pygmy within a few feet by producing a squeaking sound if the "squeaker" remains motionless. In coming toward a sound (supposedly to satisfy its curiosity), there usually develops in this little owl an excitement amounting almost to alarm. As it finds an adjacent perch on which to sit, it usually becomes greatly agitated, shifting its tail from side to side and even lifting the tail to an erect position. All the time it is bobbing and shaking its head from side to side. Altogether, its behavior looks like a combination of agitation, fear, and curiosity.

Bent (1938) states that this small owl has a well-earned reputation for courage, fearlessness, and fine hunting ability. Many ornithologists speak of it as bloodthirsty, a fiend, and a "rapacious villain." On the other hand, Bent goes on to say, "I do not know that anyone accuses this owl of killing more than it needs and when it finds its prey it strikes quickly and fearlessly, it does not cause needless suffering." Dawson (1909) states that:

Save to the few initiates a meeting with this fascinating little fiend must come as a happy accident. Fiend he is from the top of his gory beak to the tips of his needle-like claws; but chances are that you will forget his gory character at sight and call him "perfectly cunning" just because he is tiny and degagé.

There is an instinct developed in many birds that lets them know what their enemies are. It may be that the number of enemies of any bird is in direct proportion to the ferocity of that bird. If this is true, the Pygmy Owl must indeed be ferocious in the eyes of many songbirds. When the owl's presence is discovered, the songbirds in the vicinity keep up a constant quarrel with the intruder in an attempt to drive it from the territory. This may mean a gathering of juncos, robins, woodpeckers, and many other birds mobbing the owl. Flett, in Taylor and Shaw (1927), writes that "I heard a battle raging (at Longmire) outside and went out to find one Pygmy Owl dead and a flock of eight or ten camp robbers led by a Steller Jay chasing another into the woods."

I have observed these little owls for many years in the woods around the Puget Sound country and in coastal Grays Harbor. I never cease to marvel at this tiny, exquisite bird sitting in all its majestic beauty on an old stump surveying its domain. At first glance it may look rather like a large, erect-postured sparrow, but watch it feed, watch it fly, or watch it look closely at you as you lure it, and you will see immediately the unique little specimen that it is.

I once kept one for a couple of years as a pet in my laboratory. He was brought to me by a deer hunter who had placed a 30-06 calibre bullet so close to the little bird sitting on a limb of a tree that the concussion made by the passing missile knocked the bird off the limb. He had a minor injury to one wing, which we carefully wrapped and splinted until it healed. In the little pen in the laboratory he became very friendly and seemed to be very contented. He would perch on my arm and even on a finger with his claws lightly wrapped around it. When he was thirsty, I could persuade him to sip water gently from the end of a glass tube. When he was hungry, he would very delicately nibble raw hamburger from the tip of my finger. I do not recall any time in my life when I developed more affection for any kind of a pet than I did for this tiny jewel. There came a day when I walked into my lab to find him dead. I believe, but cannot prove, that he died because I could not balance his diet correctly. I think now that I did not have enough feathers, hair, and bones in his diet. Ejection of pellets may be a physiologic necessity above and beyond simply getting rid of those undigestible parts because they are there. My little owl friend was eventually prepared as a museum skin and now occupies an honored place in the museum cabinet side by side with other owls.

"OLYMPIC OWL"—
Inclusion (and Digression!)

In talking through the years with old-timers in the Northwest and others who have lived in the back country most of their lives, I am constantly impressed by the intense interest in owls—especially small owls—shown by many of these people. For more than four decades I have talked to and corresponded with the late Mrs. Lena Huelsdonk Fletcher, the daughter of one of the Northwest's most famous homesteaders. Born in a log cabin fashioned by her father in the 1890s in the rain forest in the great valley of the Hoh, my friend studied owls all her life on or near the old homestead. For more than forty years she insisted that there was, in her younger years, a tiny owl inhabitant of the fir, cedar, and spruce forests. Here the giant trees are ornamented with a drapery of moss and ferns kept moist(!) by 150 or more inches of annual rainfall.

I mention her and her experiences here because I constantly, through the years, tried to persuade her that she had been observing either a Pygmy Owl or an immature Saw-whet. She would vigorously have none of my argument, insisting that she knew the Pygmy with its two false "eyes" and the Saw-whet with its flattish head. Her owl was two thirds the size of these other small owls and "twitchy"—as are both the Pygmy and Saw-whet.

In a note, Mrs. Fletcher describes "The Owl" and its behavior with a bat:

> We had a great big snag, a dead spruce in our calf pasture, that had started as a sapling on a huge old stump and had encompassed it with its roots as it grew. Someone had tried to burn down the overgrown tree, but all that happened was that the old stump burned out and the tree stood there with a great hollow under it, a hollow that extended some 30 feet upward into the snag. It made a wonderful bat roost and also a source of charcoal for the forge to work over farm tools with. I, about 10 or 11 years old, was very intrigued by the swarms of native bats that would take to the air whenever Father with a long pole knocked down some charcoal for his work. I did so want a closer look at the bats so mother told me, "here is a dish towel. This evening when the bats fly, stand at the corner of the barn and flip one down into the grass and pick it up by the skin of its back where it can't bite you, for it is poison." (Apparently people in Europe knew early about rabid bats.) So I did as she suggested and flipped a bat flat on the grass and cautiously started to reach for it when a wren owl, never minding me or my reaching hand pounced on the bat, killed it with a couple

of skull crushing bites and then sat glaring in defiance. Satisfied that I wouldn't dispute his claim, for I had jerked back my hand, the little bird tried to carry off his prey but couldn't rise with it so he dragged it to the nearby fence brace along it to the corner post top and then flew off into the unmowed grass.

Mrs. Fletcher describes the incident of a Pygmy behaving in a way similar to "her" owl:

We, Fred and I, had just driven our cattle up an unused logging road where there was plenty elk (clear) fern to graze until snowfall. We were placing a barrier on a bridge to prevent their return to the bottom lands soon to be bare as deciduous plants winterized. There was a swamp a short distance down the road from the bridge and that had been planked over to allow passage of boards and equipment. As we stood at the bridge we heard a distinct thump on the swamp planking so, curious, we went to see. A pygmy owl was killing a big fat water vole (about the size of a mole) which then was very common along streams and is around even today. (Pampered house cats even prefer them.) Now the pygmy owl attempted to fly off with his vole, but like the wren owl with his bat he could not get up. So he too dragged his victim to a slanting route, this time the foot of a stump (spraddled out from it) then to the top of the stump and from there fifty feet away into the salal berry bushes.

I reminded my friend that there are many instances of the Pygmy Owl—when overzealous in grasping prey and unable to loosen its claw hold—dying alongside of its proposed meal.

In spite of our amiable and friendly discussion, she always insisted that in her younger years she lived with this tiny owl. It is noteworthy that a number of other old inhabitants of the rain forest area west of the Olympic Mountains—all knowledgeable about Northwest birds but most of whom are unknown to each other—tell me about this small owl with remarkable clarity and unanimity about its size, behavior, distribution, and color. As a scientist, I have great difficulty in reconciling the positive opinions about this bird given to me by talented observers where there is a lack of tangible, physical evidence such as a picture, feathers, skull, or foot that might substantiate claims. All of my old friends give the same evidence, but none gives me "in the hand" proof! If, indeed, this unique "Olympic Owl" ever existed, it seems sure that it is now extinct since no specimen has been seen in the last thirty years. At any rate, here is an example of the intense interest and involvement of people over many years living with and observing owls.

FERRUGINOUS PYGMY OWL

Glaucidium brasilianum (Gmelin)

Brasilianum is the Latinization of "Brazil"—the type locality of this species. It ranges across Mexico and along the coast through Central America, Brazil, Argentina, and extreme southwestern South America. In its northern range, it is found in southern Texas and southern Arizona. It actually extends north to the vicinity of Tucson and east as far as Brownsville, Texas.

The Ferruginous Owl is about the same size as the other Pygmy Owls, 16 to 17 cm (6½-7 in.). A specimen in the hand shows white on the upper breast and chin and brown stripes on white underparts. The back is a solid light brown with a few white feather tips above the wings. Spots on the nape of the neck appear to be "eyes." The top of the head is also light brown (ferruginous) with light-colored feather shafts giving the impression of light pencil stripes. These "pencil stripes" are more pronounced than those in the Northern Pygmy Owl. The tail is a rich reddish brown and, unlike that of the Northern Pygmy Owl, is black-barred. The beak tends to be large and considerably sharper than that of the Northern Pygmy Owl. The nails—as in other Pygmy Owls—are long, curved, and sharp. The toes and legs are sparsely feathered, and the fimbriae on the leading primaries are not highly developed.

As do most other owls, the Ferruginous Owl finds an abandoned woodpecker's hole in which to place its eggs. There is no lining, and the eggs are placed in the bottom of the cavity without any nesting material. Three to four eggs comprise a normal clutch; occasionally, there will be five in the set. The eggs of the Ferruginous Owl are somewhat different from the eggs of other Pygmy Owls. The shells are much thicker and not as smooth, and are rather coarsely granulated. They measure 24 to 29 mm by 24 to 29 mm.

There are references in the literature to the unusual prowess displayed by the Ferruginous Owl in catching and carrying off its prey. One reference by Bendire (1892) states that the Ferruginous Pygmy Owl has been known to carry off young chickens and that it has been seen to attack other fowl of greater size than the domestic chicken. In view of the small size and ferocity of the Ferruginous Owl, one might not doubt the attack example; but one could question the ability of such a small bird to carry off a bird the size of a young chicken.

Gilman (1909) relates an experience he had with a Ferruginous Owl that he wanted to capture as she sat on the nest in an old woodpecker hole. Gilman writes:

FIGURE 35.
Ferruginous Pygmy Owl.

A big handkerchief was thrust down the hole while I enlarged it sufficiently to insert my hand and arm. When my hand reached the bottom I thought it was in contact with a live wire, and I was absolutely sure I had "grabbed a live one."

When the hand was withdrawn the owl came along quite easily. One claw was through the nail of my finger, another imbedded in my big finger, while her beak was thrust deep into my thumb. Blood was running from all three wounds, and the bird hung on like a bulldog. It took no little diplomacy to remove her without forming an entangling alliance with the other hand, but she was finally safe in a handkerchief. I will back one of these owls in a rough and tumble fight with anything twice the size.

ELF OWL
Micrathene whitneyi (Cooper)

The term *Micrathene* literally means "small Athene." This is another reference associating the owl with the goddess of wisdom. The *micra-* part of the genus name alludes to the diminutive size of the Elf Owl. It is the smallest of our owls, measuring 11 to 13 cm (4½ to 5 in.). The species is named for Josiah Whitney, an early American geologist. Whitney was born in Massachusetts in 1819 and died in New Hampshire in 1896. He spent several years in California working on a geological survey of that state. Mount Whitney is named in his honor. Some of his most valuable material appeared in the Pacific Railroad reports in the 1850s.

The Elf Owl occupies the desert area and the drier deciduous-tree zones of southeastern California, Arizona, New Mexico, southern Texas, Baja California, and into central Mexico. In the plateaus and river bottoms of the southwestern United States the Elf Owl is one of the commonest birds. It likes the hot, dry lower Sonoran plains of Arizona where it is the most abundant of all its range. It favors the brushy ravines and canyons, but its nests are almost always confined to the saguaro cactus. The Elf is also found, however, in cottonwoods along the river banks at considerable distances from any stand of cactus and in sycamore in the mountains at elevations up to 6000 feet. One egg clutch, collected near Blythe, California in April, was taken from a hole in a willow tree.

The nests are usually found in the abandoned holes of flickers and woodpeckers in the giant sentinels of saguaro cactus plants. The pulp of the cactus is rather soft so that it is not difficult for a flicker or woodpecker to hollow out a nest cavity. When this happens, scar tissue builds up over a period of time around the entrance and lines the cavity. This scar tissue is harder and more persistent than the original pulp tissue, so that the cavity does not become obliterated but makes an ideal "nest box" for a number of desert birds. The one shown (Figure 37) was picked from the ground after all the tissue (except the skeleton) of the plant had decayed. This cavity is a favorite nesting place of the owl. There is considerable competition with other desert birds for these nesting holes, but the owl can and does meet this competition in spite of its diminuitive size. Woodpeckers and Elf Owls have been seen nesting in the same saguaro plant.

In keeping with its desert habitat, the Elf Owl tends to be light brown with fine spots on the back and crown, but on the breast it is lighter, with a distinct gray cast, so that the bird blends into the light desert landscape.

The Elf Owl usually lays three or four eggs but will lay any number from two to five. They do not tend to be

FIGURE 36. Elf Owl.

FIGURE 37.
Elf Owl nest hole in cactus.

FIGURE 38. Eggs of the Elf Owl.

as roundish as do many other owl eggs, and they measure 22 to 27 mm by 22 to 28 mm. Incubation begins as soon as the first egg is laid and is of rather short duration, lasting only about two weeks. Since the incubation time is short, the newly hatched owl is very small. In a few days after hatching, the white down is replaced with another downy coat that is buff in color. The molting process involving this second down coat begins in June and July. It is completely replaced by the last part of September, when the first complete set of adult feathers appears on the bird.

The food of the Elf Owl is limited almost entirely to insects and larvae, such as grasshoppers, beetles, and crickets, that abound in the desert. There are records of bird feathers appearing in the stomachs of the Elf Owls, but these records are few and probably indicate that the Elf Owl is much less aggressive than the Pygmy or other small owls. It lives compatibly with other birds in its desert environment.

The Elf Owl is almost completely nocturnal. It prefers to sleep during the heat of the day and feed at nighttime, as the warmth of the night keeps the insects active. It tends to stay away from the cactus in which it nests other than during the nesting season. In the lighter desert evenings and nighttime it can be seen flying about, capturing insects on the wing.

BURROWING OWL
Athene cunicularia (Molina)

Athene was the goddess of wisdom. The old genus name *Speotyto* is from the Greek *speo-*, meaning "cave" or "excavation," and *tyto* is Greek for a species of owl. *Cunicularia* is from the Latin meaning a "miner" or "burrower," since *cuniculus* is a pit or a hole. Here is a classic example of a taxonomist using a Greek term for the genus and a Latin term for the species, and both the generic and specific terms refer to the same characteristic! Obviously, the meaning of the scientific name refers to the fact that the Burrowing Owl spends part of its life underground. The Burrowing Owl is, incidentally, one of the few land birds that chooses a subterranean nest site.

Juan Ignacio Molina was a naturalist born in Chile in 1740. He was the author of several books, including

Flora of Chile in 1782 and later studies on the history, geography, and natural resources of Chile. He died in Imola, Italy in 1829.

The Burrowing Owl, often called the "comic of the plains," is a bird of the New World. It inhabits the open country of Western North America and all of South America in suitable localities, except for the jungles of Brazil. They are found in the plains and prairies west of the Mississippi Valley to the Pacific from southern Canada through Mexico. There is a small population in southern Florida. It prefers the open plains not given over to cultivation and agriculture.

The distribution of the Burrowing Owl is unusual. While it likes the open prairies of western America, there is also a population in the humid areas along the Pacific Ocean. I have examined live birds and skins of Burrowing Owls from the mouth of the Fraser River in western British Columbia to as far south as the Channel Islands off the Santa Barbara, California coast. It seems out of character to see Burrowing Owls in the wet, coastal regions of northwest Oregon, Washington, and British Columbia. Since humid, coastal areas tend to darken plumages in various races of birds, it is not surprising that the colonies of Burrowing Owls found along the Washington and Oregon coasts are very dark compared with the prairies' and plains' populations. I have in hand a Burrowing Owl skin taken on Moon Island in the center of Grays Harbor in the state of Washington. This specimen has a very obscure throat patch of white. The brown is a dark buff, almost chocolate color, especially over the wings and back. The white spots of the plains birds are also very obscure, but in the coastal specimen the underparts are gray and are rather faintly barred. It is, in overall coloration, much darker than the eastern Washington and eastern Oregon specimens. This dark

FIGURE 39. Burrowing Owl.

plumage is evident in all the extreme coastal Burrowing Owls from British Columbia through Oregon. Southern coastal specimens are lighter than coastal Washington specimens but darker than inland forms. Burrowing Owls in northern latitudes tend to migrate during harsh winter months, but in some northern areas small populations may winter over in the nesting grounds if food remains plentiful. The birds are more gregarious in winter.

The Burrowing Owl measures 22 to 25 cm (9 to 10 in.). It is long-legged and sits upright on a fence post, a convenient rock, or a hummock of ground. The shanks and toes are but sparsely feathered. There are no ear tufts, and the facial disc is more obscure than in many other owls. The adult plumage is a buffy brown with considerable white on the underparts, which gives it the appearance of being spotted on the upper breast and barred on the abdomen and flanks. There is a large semilunar white area on the upper breast and chin.

Dawson (1909) states that:

> On the Great Plains they avail themselves largely of deserted prairie dog holes. In the northwest their choice lies between the holes of squirrels or badgers if in the open sage, but limited to gopher holes in the close-cropped prairie land....A typical burrow may descend sharply three or four feet then bend and rise gently until an ample nesting chamber a foot or more in width and six inches deep is reached.

The Burrowing Owl usually does not build its own burrows, but it may enlarge a tunnel made by a small rodent. Of all the available burrows, this owl prefers an old badger hole. The bird digs not with its beak but with its powerful claws loosening the dirt, kicking it backwards by successive stages until the soil is ejected at the entrance. Bent (1938) states, "It loves the virgin prairies and the unbroken plains but does not take kindly to cultivated land; consequently the encroachment of agriculture has greatly restricted its former range." This may be one reason why this owl is becoming scarce. Owl populations also may have been sharply decreased by the use of sulphur compounds to kill ground squirrels. Farmers poisoned all holes indiscriminately, thus killing many owls. Indeed, it can probably be legitimately classified as rare and endangered in America.

Due to the Burrowing Owl's habit of spending much of its time under the ground (especially during the nesting season), many stories and tall tales about the bird have sprung up. As far back as 1874, Coues tried to explain the basis for some of these stories. A few of these tales are built around the supposedly happy family relationships the owls have with prairie dogs and rattlesnakes in the holes made by ground squirrels and prairie dogs. Coues says:

> First as to the reptiles it may be observed that they are like other rattlesnakes, dangerous venomous creatures. They have no business in the burrows and are after no good when they do enter. They wriggle into the holes partly because there's no other place for them to crawl into on the bare flat plain and partly in search of owl eggs, owlettes, and puppies to eat. The owls themselves are simply attracted to the villages of the prairie dogs as the most convenient places for shelter and nidification where they find eligible, ready-made burrows and are spared the trouble of digging for themselves. A community of interest makes the owls gregarious to an extent unusual among rapacious birds; while the exigencies of life on the plains cast their lot with the rodents. The probability is that young dogs often furnish a meal to the owls and in return the latter are often robbed of their eggs while certainly the young of both and the owl's eggs

are eaten by the snakes. It is in "deserted villages" that the owls are usually seen in the greatest numbers.

The nesting cavity may be at the end of a tunnel as long as ten feet. The cavity is lined with various materials such as feathers and dung brought in from the outside. The entire tunnel may contain much of the same type of material that is brought into the nesting cavity. Over a period of years, the same burrow may be used; it may be cleaned out and repaired from one year to the next. The burrows may be found on level ground or may be on a hillside or on the gradual slope of a hill. The tunnels are about five to six inches in diameter, and the nesting cavity may be anywhere from a foot to eighteen inches wide. Bendire (1892), discussing the nesting of the Burrowing Owl in northern Idaho, states that dry horse and cow manure broken up in small pieces is brought to the nesting chamber and spread out to line the floor of the cavity for a thickness of one to two inches. He further states that he has never found any other material in any of the northern Idaho nests. In data covering three sets of Burrowing Owl eggs is the following: "Entire tunnel 7 ft. long well spread with horse dung"; "Entrance, entire runway and nest of horse dung"; and "Nest, tunnel and mound well spread with dung and wool." The principle enemy of the Burrowing Owl is the badger, and the presence of dung in the nest cavity may serve to mask the odor of nest and young.

When I have dug out owl burrows in recent years (with students doing the work!), we are constantly amazed at the great amounts of manure brought to the nest chambers. This is all the more astonishing when we realize that in this modern day of mechanical farming, with combines no longer horse-drawn, the owls must range far and wide to find large quantities of their "favorite" nesting materials. They will substitute cow dung in place of their favorite—horse dung.

On the "good" habits of the Burrowing Owl, a sentence or two quoted from Dawson (1909) is revealing. Dawson remarks:

> One need not kill these Owls to learn what they feed on, for half-eaten mice, dismembered frogs, and headless snakes litter the floor, and invite the offices of the far-venturing blow-fly. Fleas usually abound; and altogether the nuptial chamber of this doughty troglodyte is not an inviting place.
>
> From six to eleven young are raised in a single brood; and when we consider that the adults themselves require more than their own weight of animal food daily, we begin to form some conception of the economic importance of these birds. Their food includes all the baneful rout of rodents, and they are able to kill "ground squirrels" of a size equal to their own. Besides these, lizards, frogs, snakes, and even small fish, are captured.
>
> Grasshoppers and crickets, as well as beetles of many sorts, are staple food, and for these the bird hunts by day as well as by night. In the pursuit of prey, however, the birds become much more active at sunset, when they may be seen flitting about on noiseless wing, or else hovering in mid air above a suspected spot, after the well known fashion of the Sparrow Hawk. Small game is snatched from the ground without lighting, but in capturing a ground squirrel, the bird first plants his talons in the back, then breaks the creature's neck by sharp quick blows of the beak. Soberly regarding the special situation of the East-side rancher, I should say that the Burrowing Owl is his best ally among birds, and that he who wantonly destroys one should be classed with the man who tramples a field of grain or sets fire to a haystack.
>
> Whenever food is plenty and the ground inviting, Burrowing Owls are likely to form little colonies, ten or a dozen pairs being found in a stretch of two or three

acres. They appear to be peaceably disposed toward each other, and mates are notably faithful. Soon after the return in spring, which occurs during the first week in March for the southern part of the State, and the first week in April for the northern, one may hear at evening a soft and mellow love song, *coo co-o,* which the male repeats by the hour. One who has heard this tender note welling up from the back pasture, while the locust trees by the gate are distilling their sweetest fragrance, and Adams [county] is fading on the western horizon in the last afterglow of sunset, can easily forgive many things about the Burrowing Owl which are less pleasant.

The food of the inland birds consists largely of small mammals and small birds, but it is quick to take other food such as lizards, toads, snakes, fish, centipedes, scorpions, and crayfish. There is evidence that the major articles of diet in the spring consist of small mammals, while insects are the most popular in the summer. This may be a matter of availability, since many mammals tend to burrow underground in the summer to escape the heat. Bendire (1892), typical of the day, called rodents "noxious vermin." The coastal colonies, although small mammals are available in great numbers, seem to prefer insects. In a note printed in the *Murrelet* (1941) on the Western Burrowing Owl in Grays Harbor County, Washington, I made the following observations. On Sand and Goose Islands in Grays Harbor, no rodents and few insects were observed and no owls, but on Moon Island, both insects and mice were abundant. In examining the stomach contents of eleven owls, I could only find the remains of beetles and other insects. While this is not a big sampling and may not be typical, I have always wondered why the Grays Harbor owls did not dine luxuriantly on the meadow voles that were found all over the island. I was never able to tell by examining pellets on

Moon Island which pellets belonged to the short-eared Owl and which to the Burrowing Owl, but I have always suspected that those containing mostly insects were the products of the Burrowing Owl and not the Short-eared.

To the best of my knowledge, no eggs of the Burrowing Owl have ever been seen in the Northwest's coastal areas. It would not appear to be too difficult for the birds to excavate a burrow in the soft sand held together by the roots of the vegetation if the coastal colonies were stimulated to nest in the area. Burrowing Owl eggs measure 24 to 26 mm by 27 to 31 mm. From six to eleven eggs comprise a clutch.

A single brood is raised in one season, and the incubation period is about three weeks. It is not uncommon to observe the parent owls eating their own egg shells. The eggs tend to become soiled during the process of incubation, but when removed from the nest and cleaned, they are exquisite geometrical objects, perfect in their oval, roundish form and pure, glossy white.

By any standards of measurement, the Burrowing Owl is a "character." While it can be raised successfully in captivity, it tends to be quiet within the confines of the aviary. It will dig, in instinctive preparation for a burrow, in the floor of the pen and will accept a pipe six to eight inches in diameter buried in the earth for its own tunnel and brooding chamber. In the wild, however, there is a constant display of clucking, bowing, and chattering. It will stand stiffly erect on a mound or an old fence post and then suddenly duck into a hole, or it will roll its eyes, twitch the muscles of wings and its face, bow, and then rise abruptly into the air. The bowing movements will go forward until the breast touches the ground. Enclosure in the aviary seems to discourage these various antics.

A number of remarkable observations have been

FIGURE 40. Eggs of the Burrowing Owl.

made on the various behavior patterns of this bird. Grinnell (1931) states:

> When the burrow had been dug out about two-thirds of the way to the end, a buzzing screech was heard that seemed so nearly like the muffled rattle of a rattle snake that it was hard to feel sure that there was no snake in the burrow. As the digging proceeded this noise was heard more and more clearly. Finally the terminal cavity was opened up disclosing only the six young owls. Their main defense was the utterance of the rasping, penetrating, rattling hiss nearly like the angry buzz of the rattle snake when disturbed on a warm day. The bill clicks which were produced less frequently than the rattling notes were rather weak. The latter utterance was deterrent in our case; might it not be so as regards carnivores that dig out or enter burrows such as the burrowing owls inhabit? Predators might thus be deterred from molesting the owls.

In 1929, Robertson gave the following account of the methods employed by these owls when feeding their young after they were large enough to come out of the nest:

> The young owls were usually in a compact group on the highest part of the mound, while the adult, only one adult being observed, had several lookout stations, the nearest one being the top of a pile of baling wire and other junk on the alkali flat, and the others were fence posts at various distances from the burrow.
> The usual program was as follows: The adult, frequently looking skyward, sighted some flying insect passing over, launched out in pursuit, climbing rather laboriously upward at a sharp angle and sometimes spirally, often to a height of 150 feet or more, and on overtaking the flying prey seized it with one foot. Then came

a pause during which the prey was transferred to the beak, then a long glide, on set wings, directly to the nest. The young, on seeing the adult coming with food, rushed down the slope toward it, and then turned and rushed back as the adult passed over their heads to alight on the highest point of the mound. Then came a scuffle that would have done credit to a football game. However, actual possession of the coveted morsel seemed to be respected, and the lucky youngster was allowed to devour it at leisure. After a brief pause the adult returned to a vantage point to watch for more game . . . .

As the young grew older and learned to fly they sometimes flew toward and intercepted the adult before the burrow was reached; this was successful only in cases where the adult flew close to the ground after making a low, or a ground, capture. The adults sometimes ate the prey themselves, and in this case it was sometimes held up to the beak with one foot while the bird stood on its perch.

Over a long period of time in observing the Burrowing Owl, various ornithologists have used a number of adjectives in describing their characteristics. These descriptions do not seem to be exceeded in any other species. Their long legs and short tails and their unbalanced position give them an element of the grotesque. They have been described as ludicrous, bland, earnest, and self-satisfied. They have been accused of bowing low with "profound gravity." Their flight is strong but of short duration because the wings tend to be short and rounded, but this owl is an expert at hovering. It flies noiselessly close above the ground in a jerky, irregular fashion. That it is a fairly good flyer, however, can be attested to by the fact that it has alighted on ships at sea some miles off shore.

In summation, the Burrowing Owl is a most interesting creature. Watching it in its native habitat or in the confines of an aviary constitutes a pleasant and educational experience. We should cherish as part of our wild heritage this fascinating and valuable bird, and we should be careful to see that its present range is not lessened or destroyed but rather that more environments suitable for its successful life cycles be made available to it.

BARRED OWL
Strix varia (Barton)

There are brown and white bars around the back of the head and the underparts of this bird, which accounts for the common name and the Latin *varia* ("variegated"). *Strix* is also derived from Latin, meaning "shrill" or "strident." Benjamin Smith Barton was an American physician and naturalist born in Lancaster, Pennsylvania in February 1766. He studied medicine in Europe but returned to practice and teach botany and medicine in Pennsylvania. In addition to being the author of the first elementary botanical text written by an American, he also published a systemic treatise on medicinal plants. He was the founder and editor of the *Philadelphia Medical and Physical Journal* from 1805 to 1808. He died in 1815.

The Barred Owl is found across southern Canada, south through Montana, Wyoming, Colorado, Texas, Louisiana, and Florida, and into the mountains of Mexico and Central America. Its southern limit is Guatemala and Honduras. In the west, it ranges into north-central British Columbia and east into Alberta. Recent records show this species is increasing in northern Idaho, Washington, and coastal Oregon. Bent (1938) states that the Barred Owl is extremely constant in its attachment to a favorite nesting site. Records have been kept showing certain pairs of owls occupying the same nest cavity over a period of many years.

The Barred Owl is a large bird, measuring 48 to 52 cm (19 to 21 in.), with a round head. Along with the Spotted Owl and the Flammulated Owl, it is the only true owl with a dark eye. The face mask of the Barred Owl is grayish, with dark but faint concentric rings. The common name of the bird is derived from the obvious barring, especially across the upper breast and neck. Vertical stripes show on the abdominal and flank regions. The entire back and tail show obvious horizontal barring.

In eastern North America, this owl inhabits the deep forest and is the most common and most abundant of all the owls there. During the day it penetrates into the deeper woods to spend its time in quiet seclusion. If it is disturbed, however, it becomes active and noisy.

The Barred Owl nests in the hollows of dead trees. The birds seem to prefer the evergreen woods rather than the deciduous forests. Quite often, the owls will choose an old hawk's nest. The eggs are laid in the cavity on the bare, rotten chips, and if the nest is used for more than one year, there may be an accumulation of rubbish. There are records of the cavity being as deep as eight feet, but it may also be very shallow. Early naturalists in America often spoke about the careless habits of

FIGURE 41. Barred Owl.

the owl in building its nest. Bent (1938) stated that he doubted that they ever succeeded in building a satisfactory nest for themselves. If they cannot find a good nest that they can appropriate, they will attempt to make one for themselves, and it usually turns out to be a very poor one. The nests are often so flimsy that they are not secure enough to retain the eggs. It is not uncommon for the eggs to roll out of the nest and be broken on the ground. There are numerous records of the Barred Owl

FIGURE 42. Eggs of the Barred Owl.

sharing a nest site with another predator, such as the hawk. On occasion, the hawk eggs and the owl eggs will both hatch. It is possible that both species share the incubation chore. Barred Owls may, on occasion, accept a nest box placed in a tree.

The Barred Owl usually lays two or three eggs, but sometimes it will lay four. The eggs are granulated and dull, not glossy, and measure approximately 43 mm by 50 mm. Incubation occupies a period of three to four weeks. Young Barred Owls are blind at hatching, but by the end of the week their eyes are open, and they begin to move around in the nest. The plumage develops rapidly, and at the end of about three weeks the familiar barred and spotted pattern of the young birds begins to show. In the autumn, the first winter plumage is developed. This will be replaced gradually by a spring plumage that is in every way adult.

The food of the Barred Owl consists of almost "anything that is edible." This includes birds, mammals, reptiles, amphibians, fishes, and insects. Mice, when available, are preferred. Some stomachs, when examined, show rather "exotic" foods, such as snails, spiders, slugs, and bats. They will, on occasion, take poultry from the chicken yard, but they seem to prefer (probably because of accessibility) songbirds, woodpeckers, and even crows. Errington (1932) states that it is his belief that the food is determined for the owl by what it is in the power of their weak feet to kill. "Altogether," he says, "the Barred Owl seems to be endowed with about as mild a personality as a raptor could have and yet maintain a predatious [sic] existence." There are instances where, for a considerable amount of time, Barred Owls have lived upon large invertebrates, such as insects and crayfish, or upon weak fish or amphibians. As an added note of interest, Errington (1930) states that in an experiment fifty-five English sparrows released alive in a cage were eaten in 154 hours by one owl. Bowles (more in Bent 1938) performed an unusual experiment with a pair of captive Barred Owls. He placed one in a barrel in which there was a "large number" of mice. One owl very quickly disposed of nineteen mice. Within six hours the entire number of mice was disposed of by the two owls. Bowles said that he could not keep owls in the sunny cellar where his chickens were, for they caught and ate some of his pullets and "terrified the survivors so that their lives were a burden." The Barred Owl is not above stooping to cannibalism, as it has been seen chasing other owls such as the Screech Owl and the Long-eared Owl.

SPOTTED OWL
Strix occidentalis (Xántus)

The Spotted Owl is resident along the Pacific coast of North America and British Columbia, east through the Rocky Mountain region from Colorado, Arizona, New Mexico, and Texas to Mexico as far as Nuevo Leon. *Occidentalis* is derived from the Latin meaning "west" or "western." John Xántus was born in Hungary in 1825. After a time in the Hungarian army, he traveled to England and in 1850 came to America. In 1855 he joined the United States Army. Most of his fieldwork in America was done in the decade from 1855 to 1864. He died in Budapest in 1894 after he had served as Director of the Zoological Garden in Budapest.

The Spotted Owl is very similar to the Barred Owl in size and habits. The size of this bird is 45 to 50 cm (18 to 20 in.). Both of these species have brown eyes, unlike the bright yellow eyes of most owls. Its overall adult plumage is brown with distinctive white spots both above and below. The Spotted Owl is a secretive bird— much more so than the Barred Owl. Both inhabit the woods and forests. The Spotted Owl, especially along the Pacific coast, keeps to the denser woods. In the western parts of the states of Washington and Oregon and the province of British Columbia, it is most commonly found in the rain forests where the thick vegetation and the towering trees tend to give it good cover. In the forested slopes of the mountains, it keeps to the canyons. It is seldom seen, due to its secretive habits, but it can be heard through the dense forest. It exhibits great curiosity when squeaking sounds are produced, and it can be drawn into the vicinity from which the sounds emanate. I have heard the Spotted Owl many times in the thick forests of the Hoh and the Quinault Rivers. Leo Couch, who was a skilled field biologist of many years' experience, has told me that he has on several occasions seen the Spotted Owl take the chipmunk that inhabits the rain forest. It was Couch's belief that the chipmunk is the major staple article of diet of the Spotted Owl. This is probably true since the small mammals that inhabit the ground are fairly scarce and difficult to acquire due to the thick understory. Also, the passerine birds that could be part of the diet of the owl are not abundant in the deep forest. Long-time residents in the Olympic Peninsula region of the state of Washington claim that the Spotted Owl is not uncommon. Its secretive habits simply make it difficult to see. There is much concern that this species may be declining in numbers in the Northwest due to the competition from logging activities. Without doubt, also, many were killed by the erup-

FIGURE 43. Spotted Owl.

tion of Mount Saint Helens in Washington State in May 1980.

The Spotted Owl will nest in the hollow of an old tree or will, on occasion, place its eggs in the old nest of another bird, such as a hawk. In its southern range, it is not uncommon for it to use a rocky cliffside. Ligon, in Bent (1938), noted that a favorite haunt of the Spotted

127

Owl in New Mexico was the caves and crevices of canyon walls. Eggs are known to have been laid on bare ground at the base of a large rock, or they may be deposited annually in the cavity of an old tree over a period of many years, suggesting that perhaps descendants of the original owls use the same nest or cavity.

A clutch is composed of two, three, or, rarely, four eggs. They are dull, white, and slightly granulated, measuring 49 to 52 mm by 41 to 43 mm. The size, composition, and shape of the eggs make them indistinguishable from those of their eastern relative, the Barred Owl. Incubation is approximately one month. A brownish second natal down worn through the summer months is replaced with a soft plumage on the underparts, which becomes spotted and barred. The first winter plumage, very similar to that of the adult, replaces this brownish down in early autumn.

Small mammals, when available, especially in the southern range, probably make up the major share of the diet. Feathers and bird bones have been found in the pellets of the Spotted Owl, but apparently, birds are eaten only when mammals are scarce or not available.

The Spotted Owl is distinctly nocturnal. During the daytime, it is deep in the woods, and it sleeps through the daylight hours. I have, on a number of occasions, disturbed the sleeping bird as I hiked along the muted, forested trails in the Quinault country in the rain forest area. The Spotted Owl is not only shy, it is also not aggressive. When disturbed, it flies quietly to an adjacent tree, moves sideways along the limb until it is close to the trunk, settles its feathers in place, and proceeds to go to sleep again. When disturbed near its eggs or young, the adult owl will commonly alight somewhere within a few feet of the intruder and will show none of the anger or fear that many other owls exhibit by hiss-

FIGURE 44. Eggs of the Spotted Owl.

ing, clapping the bill, or even striking with their talons. All in all, this is a shy, quiet bird, and it has been classified as "a bird with mild stupidity." In spite of this, there is an instinctive dislike on the part of many other birds for the mild-mannered Spotted Owl. If one is observed by other birds, there is an excited chattering and swooping to disturb the owl. The woodpeckers and the aggressive jays especially take great delight in flying at the bird in an instinctive message of dislike.

The race of Spotted Owl that inhabits the north Pacific coast is a truly striking bird. Its plumage seems to be especially soft and velvety, and since it inhabits the coastal regions, this plumage is affected by the humid zone and is darkened to a rich, vibrant brown. The large head without ear tufts and the soft, glowing feathers with the richness of the color and the pattern of the spots make this owl an exquisite bird.

GREAT GRAY OWL
Strix nebulosa (Forster)

Nebulosa is from the Latin for "cloudy" and probably refers to the light and dark gray overall plumage of this large bird. Coues (1874), with great imagination, carries the origin of the name a little further in that he says that other forms of *nebulosa* are *nubes*, "cloud," *nubo*, "I marry," and *nebulose*, "marriageable," the bride being veiled *(nupta)* for the nuptials! Johann Reinhold Forster was a German naturalist born in Dirschau, East Prussia in October 1729. A scholar with an M.D., a Ph.D., and a Doctorate of Civil Law, he emigrated to England and taught languages and was a writer and a translator. As the naturalist on Cooke's second expedition (1772 to

1775), he described seventy-five new genera of plants. He also wrote several works in the fields of history and natural history. He died in 1778.

The Great Gray Owl is circumpolar in distribution, and in North America, it is found from the tree line in Alaska, south along the coast through Washington, the mountains of California, Idaho, Montana, and Wyoming. In Canada, it spreads across the provinces through Ontario. It is weakly migratory and has been found along the Atlantic coast as far south as Massachusetts and New York. The winter period is usually spent in its breeding range.

The Great Gray Owl has been said to be the largest of all the owls, measuring 63 to 68 cm (25 to 27 in.). Actually, it weighs less than the Snowy Owl or the Great Horned Owl and is only slightly heavier than the Spotted Owl. The Great Gray Owl has long wings, a long tail, a large, round head, and a big facial disc with concentric rings, giving the impression that it is a very large bird with small eyes. The body is small, surrounded by a great collection of soft feathers. This discrepancy in appearance and actual size was first noted by Elfrig (1906), who said:

> The body taken from this owl (that is trunk without skin), head and wings measured in length only six and a half inches, depth from the breast bone to the back, 3 3/8 inches, width across the thorax 2 1/2 inches and weighed 8-10 oz. . . . It is hard to understand how such a tiny body compared to the bulk of the bird could keep up the huge wings, heavy claws, and heavy head whose circumference measures twenty inches. Facial disc alone is six inches.

The wingspread measures up to 60 inches, and the tail is 11 to 13 inches. The maximum weight of the entire bird is less than three pounds.

FIGURE 45. Great Gray Owl.

This owl has long intrigued naturalists. One was shot in June of 1854 near Willapa Bay (in coastal Washington) by Dr. Cooper, who described the spot as a "brackish meadow partially covered by small spruce trees." There are other records as far back as 1892 of this owl inhabiting the spruce trees bordering the Pacific Ocean, within one mile of the salt water.

I have seen this bird a few times in northern Washington and in southern British Columbia. This species consistently shows little fear, and an observer is permitted by the bird to approach to within a very short distance. The Great Gray Owls that I have seen are largely nocturnal. On sunny days, this owl penetrates the woods and sits quietly with its eyes half closed, waiting out the day even though it may be shadowy under the canopy of trees. On the forest borders it behaves the same way. No matter what the amount of light, it sits quietly, its eyes mere slits, reluctant to move away or even to recognize that some foreign animal, such as a human, has invaded its domain. For the Great Gray Owl in the north country, its behavior is quite diurnal. Here it will be abroad during many daylight hours because in the summer period there is very little darkness, but by choice, it will hunt here during darkened hours also. It is a low flyer, generally keeping within twenty feet of the ground.

The Great Gray Owl builds a nest in any convenient and suitable tree or snag. The nest is composed of sticks with a sparse lining of feathers and down. It may appropriate an old hawk's nest for its own use and will leave whatever material the hawks brought in to serve its own purposes. Nests may be placed at a considerable distance above the ground, perhaps at 50 feet or more. The usual number of eggs is three, but it may lay as many as five. The eggs are oval and measure 43 to 45 mm by 48 to 52 mm. The shell is dull white and granulated, giving it a

FIGURE 46. Eggs of the Great Gray Owl.

rough appearance. The young hatch after an incubation period of about a month and first assume the white natal down, which is covered within a few weeks with dark brown down. By August, the wings and tail are well developed and the grayish-white color of the adult begins to appear. By September, the young are quite fully grown, with subadult plumage. There may be an additional molt in the middle of the winter season. If so, the winter feathers are replaced by plumage that is almost completely adult.

The Great Gray Owl prefers to feed upon small mammals such as rats, mice, squirrels, rabbits, and gophers. It is a source of wonder that this gentle owl, so big and yet so small, can manage to kill and carry away an animal the size of a hare. The killing of squirrels seems to be about the usual limit of the physical ability of the owl. On occasions, this owl will capture and eat small birds. But either by choice of appetite or availability, birds do not seem to form the principle food of the Great Gray.

LONG-EARED OWL
Asio otus (Linnaeus)

Both generic and specific terms are from the Latin meaning "Horned Owl," although Coues (1874) states that
Asio may be of Hebrew origin rather than Latin. The
Long-eared Owl, measuring 35 to 40 cm (14 to 16 in.), is
found around the world in the Northern Hemisphere
from the British Isles and Siberia south to northern Europe, east to the Himalayas, and north through the Oriental countries; in North America, it is found as far
south as Arizona, Texas, Oklahoma, Arkansas, Virginia,

and Florida. It is not highly migratory, and the winter range is approximately that of the breeding range. Strangely enough, this species is accidental in southeastern Alaska, while it is a fairly common breeding bird in the southern Mackenzie region of Canada near Fort Simpson and Fort Providence, where the Mackenzie River springs from the Great Slave Lake in the Northwest Territories. It is likewise strange that the Long-eared Owl is sometimes found in some habitats that seem not to fit the bird. It may be seen along stream banks and in the central part of its range in the desert country. It will live where there are groves of evergreen trees or wherever deciduous trees are thick and dense. These habitats conform to its life cycle, since the trees will be used for nesting in the breeding season and concealment during the day. So the bird is equally at home in the northland, around deep groves of coniferous trees, and in the forest areas of Central America and the deserts of the Southwest. It also tends to be gregarious, so that it is not uncommon to see fairly large groups of Long-eared Owls living and flying together. It is largely nocturnal in its habits, spending the day in a convenient cover for protection. The behavior of this owl, together with its striking design of concealing coloration, often makes it very difficult to see in its native habitat.

The Long-eared Owl will use an old bird's nest or an old squirrel's nest for depositing its eggs. While it may add to the sticks and rubbish, it is not particular about cleaning up the old nest that is appropriated. I have before me two sets of eggs of the Long-eared Owl, a set of five and a set of six. A moment's reflection of years ago: The time was the middle of March. The slim, immaculate Long-eared female, with long ear tufts erect, quietly but daintily left her nest in a clump of willows. She flew to a nearby perch on a tree and silently watched me as I proceeded to carefully examine the

FIGURE 47. Long-eared Owl.

fresh eggs in the nest. I had some reservations (as I always do) about robbing this beautiful creature of these exquisite eggs, immaculate white with a smooth and glossy shell. I either reconciled or justified my action by the early date of the season. March was early for birds to lay in this latitude, but I knew that this mother owl would proceed immediately to the production of another set of eggs to replace the ones she lost. On another date, March 24, we disrupted the female on a set of five, laid in an old magpie's nest that had lost its top. This nest, likewise, was in a clump of bushes but this time in a canyon at the base of some dry foothills.

The Long-eared Owl's clutch usually numbers four or five, but it can lay as many as eight eggs and bring up all eight young. The eggs are oval and measure 32 to 33 mm by 39 to 42 mm. The incubation period tends to be somewhat shorter in the Long-eared Owl than in some other owls and may extend to something slightly over three weeks. Again, as in most other owls, an egg is laid every other day, with incubation beginning immediately. If there are eight eggs in one nest, the first owl hatched is much older than the last one hatched. This means that the latecomer suffers competition in the nest when food is brought to the young by the adult birds. Young birds will be able to fly at the age of about two months, at which time they can usually hunt for themselves. In the autumn there is usually a molt, to be replaced by adult feathers in early winter.

The favorite foods of the Long-eared Owl are small mammals, especially small rodents. If necessary, this owl will feed on other birds, but mammals up to the size of rabbits will be accepted. Occasionally, insects are eaten, but pellet examination shows that field mice are preferred. Since availability of various prey is related to season, there may be a drop in the percentage of small mammals found in Long-eared Owl diets through the winter and into the spring. If other birds are found in their pellets, it is usually during the time when the young owls are being fed. With five or more hungry mouths to feed, the adult birds, from necessity, turn to whatever food is accessible, be it mammal or small bird.

The Long-eared Owl is largely nocturnal, but during the season when it is necessary to feed young, it holds forth during the daytime to bring food to the nestlings.

FIGURE 48. Eggs of the Long-eared Owl.

Naturalists agree that it is one of the most bold and demonstrative owls when the young are threatened or when someone approaches the nest containing the young. Bent (1938) states that on one occasion, when he had disturbed a female and she had flown from the nest:

> Her cries of distress soon brought her mate to the scene and the performance began. Both parents were very demonstrative, flying about close at hand, alighting in the tree close to me, threatening to attack me and indulging in a long line of owl profanity.

The Long-eared Owl is one of a few owls that will attempt to entice strangers away from a nest by an instinctive behavior common to many other birds. This behavior, not found in very many owls, appears to be out of place. When alarmed or frightened, the owls will drop to the ground as if wounded and will flutter across the terrain as if a broken wing made it impossible to fly. All the time, there will be a crying and a fluttering just ahead of the pursuer. This wounded-bird act, so common in shore birds and gallinaceous birds, is a rarity among birds of prey. Dawson in 1923 described the enticement behavior:

> The male parent had delivered himself of his strange objurgations and had retired from the scene in disgust. The female had caterwauled and conjoled and exploded and entreated by turns, all in vain....All of a sudden the Owl left her perch, flew to some distance and pounced upon the ground, where she could not well be seen through the intervening foliage. Upon the instant of the pounce, arose the piercing cries of a creature in distress, and I, supposing that the bird in anger had fallen upon a harmless Flicker which I knew dwelt in that neck of the woods, scrambled down instantly and hurried forward. The prompt binoculars revealed neither Flicker nor mouse. There was nothing whatever in the owl's talons. The victor and victim were one and the same, and I was the dupe. Yet so completely was the play carried out that the bird fluttered her wings and trod vigorously, with a rocking motion, as though sinking her claws deeply into a victim.

The flight of the Long-eared Owl over open terrain is a thing of beauty. The owl is light and noiseless, but it has wings and tail in fine mathematical proportion to the body. In most owls, the act of gliding is a rarity; it is a common action in the Long-eared Owl.

SHORT-EARED OWL

Asio flammeus (Pontoppidan)

The specific *flammeus* refers to the reddish-brown color of the Short-eared Owl. Pontoppidan was born in Norway in 1698 and early in his career became the Bishop of Bergen. He published a modification and explanation of the *Little Catechism of Luther.* He also wrote extensively about the people of his diocese. His long time interest, however, was in the natural history of Norway. He died in his homeland in 1764.

The Short-eared Owl is found throughout all of North and South America, except for parts of Mexico and the southern half of South America. It ranges across

Europe, Siberia, and the Oriental countries and is common from Iceland through Scandinavia and south into Spain and Italy in the Old World. In the New World, it ranges from Alaska across Canada, south to California, Utah, and southeastern America. It inhabits many islands of the world, including the Galapagos, Puerto Rico, and the Hawaiian group. It is found on every continent except Australia.

The Short-eared Owl's nest is placed upon the ground. There may be a few blades of grass and feathers, but often the eggs may be laid on the bare sand. The usual clutch size is five, six, or seven. The eggs are oval and measure 30 to 32 mm by 40 to 42 mm. The egg is pure white, without gloss, and is incubated for about three weeks. During incubation, the adults, when disturbed, are quick to protest any intrusive disturbance by shrill, agitated cries and an elaborate performance of the "broken-wing act." The young are hatched with the white natal down, which soon gives way to a dark brown down. The young take to the air earlier than most owls and will fly at the age of about one month. The first winter plumage develops in the autumn and is almost like that of the adult. Adult birds measure 28 to 33 cm (13 to 15 in.).

The food of the Short-eared Owl consists of field mice with a sprinkling of other mammals, insects, and other birds. Occasionally, the owl will take a rabbit, and sometimes, when it is living in a dune area not too far from colonies of nesting sea birds, the owls will feed upon their young. William Brewster, in Bent (1938), noted that Short-eared Owls preyed upon an adjacent colony of nesting terns along the coast of Massachusetts. Judging from the remains, the small colony of owls had eaten at least 100 tern chicks. This is, of course, an unusual incident and does not follow the normal pattern of this owl. Observing the Short-eared on dune and estuary

FIGURE 49. Eggs of the Short-eared Owl.

for many years, I have never noticed them showing much interest in other birds as prey items. Perhaps the abundance of small mammals and ease of capture dictates the diet of this bird. There are large gull and tern colonies on islands and dunes in Short-eared country in western Washington, but no incompatibility exists there between sea birds and owls.

FIGURE 50. Short-eared Owl.

I have strong recollections of observing the Short-eared Owls over a long period of time on some of the dune islands in and around the harbors along the coast of Washington. One end of one island was covered with a thick, vegetative growth of *Phragmites,* a tall endemic grass. This gave the impression of a miniature bamboo thicket, since the grass was ten feet tall or more. There were many owls on this island, and every drift log had its quota of owl pellets. The thick mat over the island, formed by the grass and dune plants, was honeycombed with the runways and burrows of the meadow vole. When the owl sat quietly near the tall grasses, there was such a mimicry of color and pattern and sufficient ruptive marks formed by the feather pattern of the bird that it became difficult to see it at any reasonable distance. It was always a colorful and rewarding experience to watch the owls as they flew a few feet above the short grass. Suddenly, with darting movements and talons extended, an owl would disappear for a few seconds into the grass and come up with a wriggling vole held tightly in one talon.

The Short-eared Owl appears to have a small head. Actually, it is "all ears." These structures are unusually large, giving this species an acute sense of hearing (see Figures 6a and 6b). On occasion, the owls, ranging over the islands searching for something to eat, will hang suspended in the air much like a merlin or kingfisher. Then, with wings closed and tail operating as an elevator, the bird will drop quickly to the ground and come up with some prey. I have a very vivid picture of this behavior, and I can still conjure up the soft breeze coming in over the salt water, the aroma of the vegetation from the thick turf, the cool pitch of the wind, and the owls wheeling, dipping, diving, or sitting quietly on a log, blending in with the environment, illustrating nature at its perfection.

BOREAL OWL
Aegolius funereus (Linnaeus)

The generic term for this bird was first used by Aristotle, supposedly his word for some kind of owl. The species is the Latin for "funeral," which alludes to the haunting, wailing cry of the bird.

The habits and life cycle of this little owl are probably the least known of any of our owls. In early American Ornithologists' Union *Check-Lists* it was known as Richardson's Owl (*Aegolius funereus richardsoni* [Bonaparte]). The sixth edition establishes the name Boreal Owl but continues to include this species in the genus established for the Saw-whet. It has been confused with the Saw-whet Owl—especially in the immature plumage. The adult bird, however, is a size larger than the Saw-whet and has a yellowish bill with distinct, roundish, white spots on the forehead. I have a specimen in hand, and I am always conscious of the overall beauty of the rich colors of this bird. The upper parts are chocolate brown, spotted with white. It has a distinct, white facial disc. The upper parts are cinnamon, mottled with white. The feet and feathers are likewise cinnamon, and the upper breast is white. There are no ear tufts. The first winter plumage appears in early autumn. This plumage is much like that of the adult. This owl measures 22 to 25 cm (9 to 10 in.).

The Boreal is a bird of the evergreen forest and woodlands across North America and in Europe and Asia. Its breeding range in North America is a wide belt across central Canada in the coniferous and hardwood forests, north through the muskeg country into northern Alaska, northern central Yukon, and the Northwest Territories. While it is largely nonmigratory, in winter it spreads irregularly across the northern United States. There are records of it in northern Montana, Minnesota, North Dakota, and northern Michigan. One specimen was collected at Bellingham, Washington on January 17, 1905.

Much information is yet to be discovered about this immaculate little owl. It is known that the clutch size varies from three to seven eggs but usually consists of about five or six. The eggs are oval, measuring 26 to 28 mm by 33 to 35 mm, and have a smooth, dull finish. In the northland, where there are no large trees, the Boreal Owl will, on occasion, prepare its own nest. It will usually, however, place its eggs in a hole in a tree that has

FIGURE 51. Boreal Owl.

FIGURE 52. Eggs of the Boreal Owl.

been made by a woodpecker, or it will accept the open nest of a songbird. The incubation period is probably about three weeks, and the Boreal, as do most other owls, begins to incubate the eggs as soon as the first one is laid. The Boreal Owl and the Saw-whet Owl are noted for their tenacious behavior in the incubation cycle of their life histories. A quote from the field notes concerning the collection of a set of the Boreal taken in 1929 in New Brunswick states that:

> The bird appeared at the nest entrance the moment the stump was tapped, but she refused to come out, and it was finally necessary to recover the eggs from under her body—a glove was used as protection against the sharp claws which she used freely.

The food of the Boreal Owl is usually small mammals. When occasion demands it, however, the bird will feed on other birds about the size of sparrows. Captive birds have shown a marked preference for mice. Two mice daily are said to be sufficient to take care of the food needs of captive Boreal Owls. Dawson (1909) states that the Eskimos call this little owl "the blind one." Due to the inability of the eye to adjust to long periods of daylight, it can easily be captured by hand. The Eskimo children make pets of them and teach the birds to change from the usual diet of mice and birds to a diet of fish.

NORTHERN
SAW-WHET OWL
Aegolius acadicus (Gmelin)

The specific name is Latin for "Acadia," which was the old name for Nova Scotia and New Brunswick. This is the type locality for the Saw-whet. The common name refers to the resemblance of the owl's noise to that made by a file sharpening saw teeth. The Saw-whet actually has a very musical whistle, especially during the breeding season. I have had many telephone calls from people who have been in the woods in April and May and have heard this musical song and have wondered what bird was calling. It is often very difficult to locate the sound, since there seems to be so much echo in the woods and brush borders occupied by the Saw-whet. This call may go on for several days, with a whole community of people wondering where and from what bird it is coming and how many birds are involved. In the springtime, during the breeding season, the Saw-whet is an indefatigable caller; probably it is an instinctive sound emanating from the male to declare his territoriality.

The Saw-whet ranges across North America from southern Alaska through the central portion of the provinces of Canada to the Atlantic coast. In the wintertime, it may be found as far south as Arizona, California, Louisiana, South Carolina, Florida, and Georgia. A few specimens have been taken in Bermuda and Newfoundland, and there is a race of Saw-whet Owls confined to the Queen Charlotte Islands in British Columbia. It can also be found in the highlands of Mexico as far south as Vera Cruz.

The Saw-whet lays four to seven eggs, with five or six being the most common number. The eggs measure 22 to 25 mm by 27 to 30 mm and tend to be roundish, dull in color, and smooth. The incubation period is about one month. The story of a set of Saw-whet Owl eggs taken in 1909 illustrates the reluctance of the female parent to leave the set when the bird is disturbed. The collector stated that "Bird came to the opening of the nest when I rapped on the tree. I stood on an old snag and collected the bird with the cleaning rod of my gun." Another Saw-whet used a devious way to enter and leave her nest cavity. This bird would never enter her nest directly, but the cavity was "open to the south—decayed heart opening had a hollow limb running 45° angle to the NE. 8 ft. long, 6 in. hollow. Owl entered and left nest through this limb although opening was large." In a large set, the hatchlings are often found in the nest with some young that are almost ready to fly. After about two weeks in the nest, the eye begins to develop

FIGURE 53. Eggs of the Saw-whet Owl.

its yellow iris, and the early white down is replaced with
a darker down at the same time that some of the body
feathers are beginning to develop. The first juvenile
plumage is complete in the autumn, at which time the
young bird can qualify as one of the most beautiful birds
in the woods. I have in hand the skin of a young Saw-
whet that graced my laboratory for a few years. Its tail is
dark brown, marked with broken horizontal stripes of
white. The underparts are a light brown, darkening to a
rich, lustrous brown on the upper breast and across the
back. The Saw-whet tends to be much less spotted than
the Boreal, and the crown has faint stripes rather than
the small, white spots on the crown of the Boreal. The
facial disc is of the same rich, dark brown, but there is a
line of white running from the base of the bill up over

FIGURE 54. Saw-whet Owl.

each eye, giving the impression of large, V-shaped eye-brows. The adult birds measure 17 to 20 cm (7 to 8 in.). The young Saw-whet is a beautiful creature.

Of all the owls, none exhibits greater curiosity or friendliness than the Saw-whet. When disturbed about its nesting site, it will fly but a few feet and watch closely as the nest is examined. On a warm evening, it will fly around a campsite and sit on a limb of a tree a short distance from a campfire. The Saw-whet Owl has been variously regarded as tame or just fearless. It can often be approached to within a few feet, and there are instances when it has been caught in hand or under a hat. Taylor and Shaw (1927) tell of an occasion when the birds' curiosity or stupidity maybe drove them into our tent. . . . What a peculiar sensation it was to awaken suddenly and hear the call of an owl sounding within six feet of one's ear, followed soon by the soft flutter of wings as the bird left the tent.

The flight of the Saw-whet has been characterized as undulating and rapid for an owl and does not show the smooth, buoyant, more graceful soaring flight of many other owls. The favorite foods of the Saw-whet Owl are mice, squirrels, shrews, bats, and other small mammals. They will, on occasion, catch small songbirds, and they are not above eating a wide variety of insects. All in all, the Saw-whet Owl is one of our most winsome birds. It has beauty, talent, character, curiosity, and personality.

CHECKLIST OF OWLS
IN NORTH AMERICA
(A.O.U. number in parentheses)

1. Common Barn Owl (*Tyto alba* [Scopoli]) (365) Length: 38–40 cm (15–16 in.). Distribution: One race in the United States; cosmopolitan, from southern Canada south into southern South America.

2. Eastern Screech Owl (*Otus asio* [Linnaeus]) (373) Length: 20–22 cm (8–9 in.). Distribution: Eighteen races of this species have been described, ranging from the southern portions of the provinces across Canada and across the United States into central Mexico.

3. Western Screech Owl (*Otus kennicottii* [Elliot]) (373.2) Length: 20–22 cm (8–9 in.). Distribution: A resident from southeastern Alaska south to the Columbia River on the Pacific coast.

4. Whiskered Owl (*Otus trichopsis* [Wagler]) (373.1) Length: 17–20 cm (7–8 in.). Distribution: One race in the United States, southeastern Arizona south into Mexico.

5. Flammulated Owl (*Otus flammeolus* [Kaup]) (374) Length: 15–17 cm (6–7 in.). Distribution: One race, western United States south into Mexico.

6. Great Horned Owl (*Bubo virginianus* [Gmelin]) (375) Length: 52–58 cm (21–23 in.). Distribution: Ten races, ranging across the United States from the southern Arctic south to southern South America.

7. Snowy Owl (*Nyctea scandiaca* [Linnaeus]) (376) Length: 50–61 cm (20–24 in.). Distribution: Across the arctic tundras of North America; irregular winter visitor, south to Mexico in winter.

8. Northern Hawk Owl (*Surnia ulula* [Linnaeus]) (377) Length: 35–40 cm (14–16 in.). Distribution: Arctic tundras across North America and to northern United States in winter.

9. Northern Pygmy Owl (*Glaucidium gnoma* [Wagler]) (379) Length: 15–16 cm (6–6½ in.). Distribution: Five races from southeastern Alaska south through the Rocky Mountains and coastal to Baja California. One race *(G. gnoma gnoma)* (379d) reaches into Central America to Guatemala.

10. Ferruginous Pygmy Owl (*Glaucidium brasilianum* [Gmelin]) (380) Length: 16–17 cm (6½–7 in.). Distribution: From southern Arizona to southern South America.

11. Elf Owl (*Micrathene whitneyi* [Cooper]) (381) Length: 11–13 cm (4½–5 in.). Distribution: From southwestern United States south into central Mexico.

12. Burrowing Owl (*Athene cunicularia* [Molina]) (378) Length: 22–25 cm (9–10 in.). Distribution: From the southern interior provinces of Canada south into coastal islands from California south to Baja California. A small, relict population formerly occupied several islands from coastal southern British Columbia south to the Columbia River.

13. Barred Owl (*Strix varia* [Barton]) (368) Length: 48–52 cm (19–21 in.). Distribution: Dense forests from southern Canada south through Central America into Honduras.

14. Spotted Owl (*Strix occidentalis* [Xántus de Vesey]) (369) Length: 45–50 cm (18–20 in.). Distribution: Three races, in forested areas from the Rocky Mountains west to the Pacific coast and south into central Mexico.

15. Great Gray Owl (*Strix nebulosa* [Forster]) (370) Length: 63–68 cm (25–27 in.). Distribution: Almost circumpolar, in the forests of northern North America and western Eurasia. The southern limits in North America are approximately the northern tier of the United States.

16. Long-eared Owl (*Asio otus* [Linnaeus]) (366) Length: 35–40 cm (14–16 in.). Distribution: Two races, from the southern portions of the Canadian provinces south to the southern states from Texas eastward. A western race is found from interior western provinces south to Baja California.

17. Short-eared Owl (*Asio flammeus* [Pontoppidan]) (367) Length: 28–33 cm (13–15 in.). Distribution: Widespread from Eurasia, northern North America south through South America and Europe. A small population is resident in the Hawaiian Islands.

18. Boreal Owl (*Aegolius funereus* [Linnaeus]) (371) Length: 22–25 cm (9–10 in.). Distribution: In North America

from the boreal provinces of Canada south to the central United States.

19. Northern Saw-whet Owl (*Aegolius acadicus* [Gmelin]) (372) Length: 17–20 cm (7–8 in.). Distribution: In North America from southern Canada across the United States and into the mountains of Mexico. A separate race of the Northern Saw-whet Owl (*A. acadicus brooksi* [Fleming]) (372a) has been described as resident on the Queen Charlotte Islands in British Columbia.

BIBLIOGRAPHY

Abbott, Charles G. *Cyclopedia of Natural History.* New York: A.L. Burt, 1888.

———. "California Spotted Owl in San Diego County, California." *The Condor* 32 (1930), 121.

———. "Another Record of the Great Gray Owl in California." *The Condor* 45 (1943), 37.

Alcorn, Gordon Dee. "The Western Burrowing Owl in Grays Harbor County, Washington." *The Murrelet* 22 (1941), 57–58.

———. "The Burrowing Owl—Comic of the Plains." *Pacific Search* 10 (1974), no. 3.

Alderson, G. "The Status of the Great Gray Owl in Southern Oregon." *The Murrelet* 41 (1960), 28.

Arrendondo, O. "The Great Predatory Birds of the Pleistocene of Cuba." *Smithson. Contri. Paleobio* 27 (1976), 169–87.

Bendire, Charles Emil. *Life Histories of North American Birds.* U.S. Natl. Mus. Spec. Bull. no. 1. Washington, D.C.: Government Printing Office, 1892.

Bent, Arthur Cleveland. *Life Histories of North American Birds of Prey,* pt. 2. U.S. Natl. Mus. Bull. no. 170. Washington, D.C.: Government Printing Office, 1938.

Bourds, E.A., and G.A. Hesterberg. "Western Burrowing Owl in Michigan." *The Wilson Bulletin* 62 (1950), 214.

Bowles, John Hooper. "The Winter Migration of 1916–17 in the Northwest." *The Condor* 19 (1917), 125–29.

Brewster, William. "Hawk Owls in New England." *The Auk* 2 (1885), 108–9.

Brodkorb, Pierce. "The Number of Feathers in Some Birds." *Q. J. Fla. Acad. Sci.* 12 (1949), 1–5.

Bunn, D.S., and others. *The Barn Owl.* Vermillion, SD: Buteo Books, 1982.

Clark, Richard J., and others. *Working Bibliography of Owls of the World*. Washington, D.C.: National Wildlife Federation, 1978.

Coues, Elliott. *Birds of the Northwest*. U.S. Geol. Surv. Terr. Misc. Publ. no. 3. Washington, D.C.: Government Printing Office, 1874.

————. *Key to North American Birds*. Boston: Estes and Laurait, 1884.

David, Armand, with E. Oustalet. *Les Oiseaux de la Chine*. Paris: Paris Museum, 1877.

Davie, Oliver. *Nests and Eggs of North American Birds*, 4th ed. Columbus, OH: Hann and Adair, 1889.

Dawson, William Leon, and John Hooper Bowles. *The Birds of Washington*, Vols. 1 and 2. Seattle: Occidental Publishing Co., 1909.

Dawson, William Leon, *The Birds of California*, Vols. 1, 2, 3, 4. Los Angeles: South Moulton Company, 1923.

Dickey, D.R. "The Nesting of the Spotted Owl." *The Condor* 16 (1914), 193–202.

Edson, J.M. "Birds of the Bellingham Bay Region." *The Auk* 25 (1908), 425–39.

Elfrig, Charles William Gustave. "The Great Gray Owl." *Ottawa Nat.* 20 (1906), 79–81.

Errington, Paul Lester. "The Pellet Analysis Method of Raptor Food Habits Study." *The Condor* 32 (1930), 292–96.

————. "Food Habits of Southern Wisconsin Raptors. Pt. I: Owls." *The Condor* 34 (1932), 176–80.

Falla, R.A., and others. *A Field Guide to the Birds of New Zealand*. Auckland: Collins Press, 1966.

Feduccia, Alan. *The Age of Birds*. Cambridge, MA: Harvard University Press, 1980.

Gabrielson, Ira N., and Stanley G. Jewett. *Birds of Oregon*. Corvalis, OR: Oregon State College Press, 1940.

————, and Frederick C. Lincoln. *The Birds of Alaska*. Harrisburg, PA: The Stackpole Co., 1959.

Gilman, Marshall French. "Some Owls along the Gila River in Arizona." *The Condor* 11 (1909), 145–50.

Glue, D.E., and R. Morgan. "Recovery of Bird Rings in Pellets and Other Prey Traces of Owls, Hawks and Falcons." *Bird Study* 24 (1977), 111–13.

Godfrey, W. *The Birds of Canada*. Nat. Mus. Canada Bull. no. 203. Ottawa: F. A. Acland, 1966.

Griffee, W.E. "An Oregon Nest of the Great Gray Owl." *The Murrelet* 40 (1959), 35.

Grinnell, Joseph. *Birds of the Kotzebue Sound Region, Alaska.* Pacific Coast Avifauna, no. 1. Santa Clara, CA: Cooper Ornithological Club, 1900.

—— and others. *Vertebrate Natural History of a Section of Northern California through the Lassen Peak Region.* Univ. of Calif. Publ. Zool., vol. 35. Berkeley: University of California Press, 1931.

Gruson, Edward S. *Check List of the World's Birds.* New York: Quadrangle/The New York Times Book Co., 1976.

Hanna, W.C. "Whitney's Elf Owl." *The Oologist* 52 (1935), 102–103.

Jewett, Stanley G. "Northwestern Saw-whet and Snowy Owls in Oregon." *The Auk* 37 (1910), 340.

—— and others. *Birds of Washington State.* Seattle: University of Washington Press, 1953.

Karalus, K.E. *The Owls of North America.* Garden City, NY: Doubleday and Co., Inc., 1974.

Michael, Charles W. "The California Spotted Owl in Yosemite Valley, California." *The Condor* 35 (1933), 202–2103.

Minot, H.D. *The Land–Birds and Game–Birds of New England.* Boston: Estes and Lauriat, 1877.

Nelson, Edward William. *Report upon Natural History Collection Made in Alaska.* U.S. Signal Service Arctic Series, no. 3. Washington, D.C.: Government Printing Office, 1887.

Norberg, R.A. "Occurrence and Independent Evolution of Bilateral Ear Asymmetry in Owls and Implications on Owl Taxonomy." *Philos. Trans. R. Soc. Biol. Sci.* 280 (1977), 375–408.

Peters, J.L. *Check List of Birds of the World,* vol. 4. Cambridge, MA: Harvard University Press, 1940.

Potter, Eloise F. "On Capitalization of Vernacular Names of Species." *The Auk* 101 (1984), 895–96.

Quinton, Michael S. "The Great Gray Owl." *National Geographic* 166 (1984), 123–36.

Rich, P.V., and D.J. Bohaska. "The World's Oldest Owl: A New Strigiform from the Paleocene of Southwestern Colorado." *Smithson. Contri. Paleobio.* 27 (1976), 87–93.

Robertson, John McBrair. "Some Observations on the Feeding Habits of the Burrowing Owl." *The Condor* 31 (1929), 38–39.

Samuels, Edward. *The Birds of New England and Adjacent States.* Boston: Noyes, Holmes and Co., 1872.

Seton, Ernest Thompson. *The Birds of Manitoba.* Proc. U.S. Nat. Mus., vol. 13. Washington, D.C.: Government Printing Office, 1890.

Simpson, M.B., Jr. "Breeding Season Record of the Saw–whet Owl from Grayson Highlands State Park, Virginia." *Raven* 47 (1976), 55–56.

Taylor, Walter Penn. "The Barn Owl in Washington State." *The Auk* 40 (1923), 123–24.

————, and William Thomas Shaw. *Mammals and Birds of Mount Rainier National Park.* Washington, D.C.: Government Printing Office, 1927.

Thorpe, W.H., and D.R. Griffin. "The Lack of Ultrasonic Components in the Flight Noise of Owls Compared with Other Birds." *Ibis* 104 (1962), 256–57.

United States War Department. *Railroad Survey,* vol. IX. Washington, D.C.: A.O.P. Nicholson, 1858.

Van Tyne, Josselyn, and Andrew J. Berger. *Fundamentals of Ornithology.* New York: John Wiley and Sons, 1959.

Welty, Joel C. *The Life of Birds.* Philadelphia: W.B. Saunders Co., 1982.

INDEX